THE INVISIBLE DON'T BUILD GREAT BUSINESSES. THE UNIGNORABLE DO.

In the digital age, being good at your job is no longer enough. To be truly successful, you must be both talented and visible. Building an authentic personal brand is the key to getting the recognition you deserve and the opportunities you dream of.

Everyone has a reputation. So why not build a reputation you love? One that is authentic, plays to your strengths and boosts your business. In *Unignorable,* Oliver Aust guides you through a 30-day process of building your personal brand online and offline. You will work on your mindset, motivation, method and message. By the end of the four weeks, you will have a tailor-made personal branding strategy and the skills required to execute it with maximum success. You will have learned how to become truly unignorable. In uncertain times, your reputation is your greatest asset.

Unignorable

Build Your Personal Brand and Boost Your Business in 30 Days

OLIVER AUST

EDITORIAL

Publisher: Oliver Aust, Eo Ipso Communications GmbH

Staff Writers: Isobel Hambleton and Sierra Stalcup

Editors: Diane Vitry, Vincent Wolff and Lena Carlson

Designer: Bianca Amorim

Printed in Berlin, Germany by

Katalogdruck Berlin

PUBLISHED BY

Eo Ipso Communications GmbH

Friedrichstraße 68, 10117 Berlin

E: oliver@oliveraust.com

W: www.oliveraust.com

Instagram: @oliveraust_

ISBN: 978-3-9821088-2-7

ALSO BY THE AUTHOR

How to Speak Like A CE.O: How Successful Leaders Communicate

Mastering Communications: How CEOs and Executives Can Build a Great Reputation in the Digital Age

CONTENTS

INTRODUCTION

A Reputation You Love

"Be so good they can't ignore you." – Steve Martin, actor.

In a TV interview in 2007, American actor and comedian Steve Martin was asked about how he became successful. His response: "Be so good they can't ignore you." It's a great answer, and it rings true. But there is a crucial part missing.

We all know plenty of people who are good – even great – at what they do, but never get the recognition they deserve. They never seem to find enough clients or get that promotion. Upon closer inspection, being good at what you do is crucial for success, but it is not the only factor in the equation.

A generation ago, letting the work speak for itself was sound advice. There was simply no need to think beyond your current employer when working in the same organisation for decades was the norm. With good work, you were pretty much assured an upward career path.

Today, it's inevitable that a large demographic of talented and hard-working individuals will be ignored. The average professional career now spans eleven roles and more of us build businesses or become entrepreneurs. Maintaining an excellent reputation between a range of companies or roles is crucial if you don't want your track record to slip between the cracks. This is even more salient in the wake of the COVID-19 pandemic and the subsequent recession.

What's missing from "be so good they can't ignore you" is that people also need to know about you and your work. But not just anyone. Not random people. You want to become a magnet to those who matter to your cause and career. Those who can move the dial.

A personal brand comes to life when you take control of your own reputation. We all have a reputation, so why not have one you love? Becoming unignorable means precisely this: to shape a reputation you love that ensures that you matter to the people that matter to you.

This book is be about building a reputation that you are in control of and a brand that will help you have the impact on the world that you desire. The concept of unignorable has become unignorable. At the same time, becoming unignorable is getting harder and harder due to the information overload we all experience. This is the premise of this book. In a world where we compete for attention, I want you to become unignorable in the right way. I want you craft a reputation that you love and I want you to become a magnet to those who matter to you.

Build a system that maximises results and energy

In this book, I outline steps you can take to create a personal brand in 30 days, online and offline. Without spending hours every day feeding the social media beast. Without pretending to be someone you are not.

I aim to convince you that the best thing for your business is to be yourself and to build a system that works for you. I share with you a tried and tested method for creating a strong online presence that will propel you towards success. I show you how to build systems to lighten the burden of building a personal brand. Systems that will help you think and act efficiently. You will understand how to place most of your effort into the tasks that mean the most for you and your business. Your system will drive you forward. It will replenish rather than drain you.

As a result of your new personal brand, you will be able to assert yourself as a mover and shaker, and charge customers and clients what you are worth. I want you to become oversubscribed so that you have the luxury of choosing the most interesting clients and projects. A compelling personal brand will attract potential clients and prove your value. It will help you gain the trust of your audience. The next time that they are seeking an expert in your field, your name will be top of mind.

It is also important that you enjoy the process. I hope that you find genuine fulfilment in this process and learn more about your values, drivers and passions, and how to use them to help others. I am not saying my approach doesn't involve work and dedication. Of course it does. But you won't dread doing it. If you follow the steps I outline in the following chapters, small wins will lead to bigger wins and you will remember that building a brand is actually a lot of fun. Becoming unignorable is a lot of fun.

Over the years, I discovered that there are a few recurring reasons why people fail in sharing their unique voice with the world: they think building a brand means they can't be themselves; they believe they have nothing to say; they are afraid of showing up in the digital space; they get on the content treadmill, churning out half-hearted LinkedIn posts or tweets. What's more, they don't enjoy it because they don't have the right strategy or system in place.

In other words, either their mindset, motivation, method or message prevents them from succeeding. They get frustrated and then stop doing the work. "It's not for me" – a limiting belief that couldn't be further from the truth. With the right mindset, motivation, method and message, everyone can build a brand and boost their business while having some fun along the way. In this book, I address all four of these aspects, giving you the tools to build the career that you dream of.

Protect yourself from uncertainty

The 2020s are filled with uncertainty. Many are worried about losing their jobs to economic recessions or artificial intelligence, failing to upskill or becoming irrelevant. There is no point in worrying. Instead, I want you to take charge of your career and build the life you want. You deserve to be unignorable.

Resilience will be more important in the future than any particular skill. Skills can be learnt and can become obsolete. Resilience stays. It's a superpower. A first-rate reputation or personal brand is a cornerstone of resilience in business. It protects us against forces that are outside of our control. You can be fired from a job, but you can't be fired from your personal brand.

Steve Martin's quote, "be so good they can't ignore you", was popularised by an excellent book by Cal Newport with the same name. The central premise of the book is that skills, not passion, determine your level of success. Newport argues that passion without career capital – for example, skills and contacts – leads to broken dreams and businesses. He has a point. But if you read this book, chances are you are already great at what you do. Now let's make sure the world knows about it.

Before you begin, head over to oliveraust.com/unignorable to get your free copy of the *Unignorable Workbook*. It is packed with exercises that guide you through the personal branding journey detailed in this book and challenge you to think deeply about how you can become truly unignorable.

In Part I, I lead you through the reasons why you should build a personal brand. There are many, but I focus on the professional and monetary benefits. If you still have reservations, I will bust some of the myths that may hold you back.

Part II walks you through the process of building a personal brand. This is a 30-day journey, and I give you the necessary steps to lay the foundations quickly, including a strategic overview of your brand and detailed insights into the different tactics available to you. We will work on a method that works and that will carry your brand forward. Thirty days works well for most, but it's okay to take less or more time, depending on your ambition and situation.

Part III shows you how to become unignorable by building your personal brand beyond the first 30 days. From public speaking to podcasting, this section gives you a wide range of ideas and advice that will elevate you to the position of a trusted advisor. By the end of this book, you will have a clear and actionable roadmap, tailor-made to cut through the noise and make you impossible to ignore.

This all sounds like a lot of effort, I know. Polished personal brands are created to make it look as if the owner of that brand has committed their life to the cause. But that is simply not true. Even as a busy CEO, I still have time to spend quality-time with family and friends and to pursue hobbies.

The effort you put into your personal brand will pay off, year after year. What people say about you and your work is a large part of the success of your business. Building a personal brand and becoming unignorable will help you draw in future customers, because they connect with you and your values. This gives you the opportunity to surprise and delight them with your hard work. As a result, word-of-mouth will spread, and your brand and reputation will grow.

Personal branding is not about adding to the noise. We are all inundated with information and entertainment. The aim of a personal brand is to add value to the lives of your customers, clients or colleagues. Most content online is of little value. Content farms churn out millions of articles that hardly answer the reader's questions. With your personal brand, you will rise above the noise and become visible.

Your personal brand has to reflect your personality if you are to become visible and truly unignorable. Soulless corporate speak is out of fashion. Authenticity wins hearts, even in the professional world of today. You have the opportunity to openly express who you really are. Unlike ten years ago, when showing personality was still largely frowned upon in the corporate world, authenticity will help you now to get noticed. Customers, recruiters, bosses, they will all appreciate learning more about you through your authentic personal brand.

Attention is a highly sought-after commodity in the digital age. By now, we all know that advertisers will pay a high price for our attention, online and offline. This trend will not die down. In overcrowded markets, gaining attention is even more valuable. Becoming unignorable and building a successful personal brand will help you cut through the noise, rise to the top of your customers' minds and reach your goals.

During this journey, you will learn how to become unignorable by being authentically yourself. Let me show you how...

PART I

BECOME A MAGNET TO THOSE WHO MATTER

You want to build a reputation you love. To fulfil your goals, you also need the right motivation, mindset and method. In the words of Jim Kwik, you are on a path to becoming limitless if you have those three. Since we are aiming to build a brand, we need to add a fourth M: message. In the first part of the book, we focus on motivation and mindset.

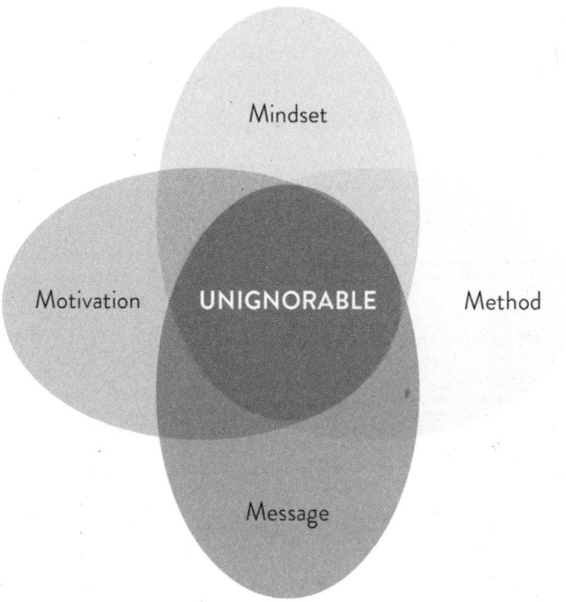

THE 4 M'S OF PERSONAL BRANDING

All four M's – mindset, motivation, method and message – are needed for a truly successful personal brand.

If your brand is consistent with your values and you set out to help others, building a personal brand should be an enjoyable and fulfilling experience. Authenticity is not just a buzzword. It is the key to understanding why some personal brands work and others don't.

In business, a great reputation is the prerequisite to profit. It separates you from your competitors. If we are known for our expertise, for being outstanding at what we do and for the value we live by and create for others, we become a magnet for the right people and opportunities. You are showing your unique self, your skills and abilities, to those who will extract value from what you have to say and share.

To be seen, we must be visible. To be heard, we must have a voice. To make an impact, we must share our vision.

CHAPTER 1

Why YOU Should Build a Personal Brand

"If you learn the ability to get your idea out into the world in a way that attracts others to join you....you're going to live a much bigger, more meaningful life." –Conor Neill, speaking coach and motivation expert.

Many professionals and business owners shrug when hearing the term *personal brand*. Most people immediately think of athletes, celebrities, Instagram influencers and maybe some larger-than-life characters like Richard Branson or Elon Musk. Sure, it makes sense for them, but for me?

Yes, it does make sense for you to create a personal brand.

Why? Hear me out.

Personal branding is not a vanity project. No longer restricted to the world of influencers and celebrities, a huge portion of today's successful entrepreneurs and professionals have an online presence of some sort. All thought-leaders have a personal brand. It is vital to reaching that status.

Jeff Bezos, Amazon founder and currently the world's wealthiest man, stated: "A brand for a company is like a reputation for a person. You earn reputation by trying to do hard things well."

As highlighted earlier, think of your personal brand as a curated version of your reputation. We all have a reputation, whether we like it or not. It consists of the thoughts that others have about us and the stories that they share. In fact, humans have an innate ability to scan for and remember reputation. Back in the hunter-gatherer days, we needed to be able to track who we could trust and who could be a threat. Those who couldn't be trusted would face the consequences. This evolutionary mechanism has made us such a co-operative species.

The way we work and live has drastically changed in the digital age. We are more mobile; we have the ability to pursue careers in different fields and organisations. Every time we make such a change, we face the challenge of rebuilding our reputation or dealing with the preconceived notions our new colleagues or industry peers have of us. And with so much information available online, it is easier for people to get to know us more than ever before.

Since we all have a reputation, it makes sense to take control of it. Why not curate the narrative so it reflects our values and achievements? In other words, why wouldn't we build a personal brand that brings the right people and possibilities into our lives and increases our chances of having a fulfilling life and career?

A quick exercise to help you gain a sense of what others think of you in a professional setting is to turn to your friends and colleagues. They know you from an outside perspective and may offer valuable insights that you had not considered.

Ask your friends and colleagues: "Why me?". Why do people want to work with you? Asking this question will inform you of how much work you need to put into changing or updating your reputation. Is your reputation right where you want it to be? Or does it need some attention?

Best-selling author and entrepreneur Seth Godin puts it this way: "Many of us are taught to do our best and then let the world decide how to judge us. I think it's better to do your best and decide how you want to be judged. And act that way."

PEOPLE BEFORE PRODUCT

There are three levels of branding: company, product and personal. Traditionally, product marketing came first, followed by company. Personal branding was often an afterthought. These days, the situation has reversed. In a world oversaturated by products and services, consumers want to support the individuals whose values or ideals they can believe in.

People will be attracted by a purpose-driven or mission-driven brand. Your purpose should be at the heart of your personal brand. Let others know what your values are. Buying a new pair of shoes is nice. But buying a pair that in turn gives a pair to someone in need? That is the model that gave rise to the TOM's brand. Why has the brand been so successful? They are adding a loftier goal to your purchase. People who believe in giving back are attracted to their purpose. Think about this when you approach your own branding. What larger purpose do you serve? Certainly, you care about more than increasing your profits.

An authentic personal brand builds context around you and your work. It gives your professional persona heart and soul. A product or service can appeal to one person at a time. A brand can appeal to whole groups of people continuously. Great brands become part of someone's identity – and can even play a role in someone's transformation. Think Nike, Weight Watchers, sports teams or luxury brands. This is also true for individuals. "They really get me," we tell our friends. And so the word spreads and businesses grow.

Context is crucial. Context in this setting refers to your values, ambitions, intentions, personality and experience. It gives your expertise depth, your qualifications meaning and your experience a purpose. It allows others to search for you and gain an immediate impression of your personality and your life up to this point. It elevates you in the minds of others, from a nebulous list of accomplishments to a well-rounded person. You create an image of a real human at the other end of the screen. More than that, you allow others to perceive you as a person with valuable insights and ideas to share, both digitally and in real life.

The best personal brands shine a light on your purpose or the benefits that you bring to the people around you. People begin to view your abstract achievements and talents in the context of their own lives or their own businesses. They look at you and consider the help or opportunities that you could bring to them. They feel part of a special club, full of others who hold the same values.

In 2011, Ella Woodward was diagnosed with a condition called Postural Tachycardia Syndrome. After spending months in hospital with strong medication, she realised there was another way out for her that did not involve pills. A plant-based diet was to be her saving grace.

Unfamiliar to cooking, she started documenting her experience on her blog deliciouslyella.com. This was an open recital of her day-to-day experience testing and trying plant-based meals. It was brutally honest and authentic. Surprising herself, she found a deep passion for plant-based living. This passion did not fall on deaf ears. Her blog started to pick up and accumulated over 130 million hits before she knew it.

Although her initial intention was to document her journey, a community grew that started to follow her on social media, flocked to her cooking classes, downloaded her app and bought her cookbooks. They too could feel the benefits of this healthier lifestyle. They connected with her and her mission. She built an expertise on the subject on the way and she is still learning today. Every product she introduces is rooted in her personal brand. Because of this, her community followed her along the way. They trusted her.

Similarly, you can share your thoughts and ideas in a way that others can practically implement. Your insider knowledge becomes impactful to your audience. More than just doing good things for yourself, you turn your successes and your expertise into value for the people around you.

You gain people's trust, and you gain their respect. You raise yourself to the status of a trusted advisor by adding genuine value to their lives without asking for anything in return. This is when your personal brand begins to pay for itself. As Daniel Priestley writes in *Oversubscribed*, "Your value is much higher than you think to a small number of people. You don't need everyone on the planet to see you in demand; you only need enough people who can drive your price up."

YOUR REPUTATION MATTERS

Maya Angelou wrote: "I've learned that people will forget what you said, people will forget what you did, but people will never forget how you made them feel." In our professional lives, those individuals who dug us out of a tough spot or gave us the advice that moved a project forward are the ones that we remember. That reputation sticks. Those brilliant mentors and friends will be top of mind when a relevant opportunity arises, or when we are asked for a recommendation. By helping others, they have helped themselves in the long run. They have formed genuine, mutually beneficial relationships based on trust and respect. These relationships are invaluable in any context.

Building a personal brand is simply developing that great reputation in a wider context. It is about helping as many relevant people as possible, knowing that your reputation will open the door to many more opportunities in the future. It encompasses sharing your wisdom, your skills and your ideas in a way that genuinely helps people. When you do this for others, they will recommend you to anyone and everyone that could benefit from your help.

You most likely already understand your clients and customers. There is great satisfaction and great value in taking the next step and establishing yourself as a true expert. A personal brand can be very profitable. In fact, building a strong brand can be essential in building career capital. The return on investment (ROI) is exceptionally high. Being seen as the go-to authority in your field is priceless.

Don't just take my word for it: Richard Branson wrote in his autobiography that he regularly appears personally in the media to strengthen his Virgin companies. Only then do the media take note. Steve Jobs' first TV interview was truly terrible and made him visibly uncomfortable. He then made the strategic decision to work on his stage presence. Over many years, this choice made him an irresistible force on stage and Apple the first trillion-dollar-company. Elon Musk is hardly a great speaker, but he understands how to garner attention and use it to build multibillion-dollar companies. All of these personalities understand their personal brand and how it helps to turn their visions into reality.

The same is true for you and your career. A strong personal brand will help you attract the opportunities you deserve. A strong personal brand sets you apart from others and is something you can take with you from job to job, business to business, from country to country. It is your multi-faceted business card that tells others about your passions and your expertise.

Is this shift from "let the work speak for itself" to "do good things and let others talk about it" a positive or negative development? You can make a case for both, but I prefer to look at the upside. Today there are more opportunities for more individuals because original thinking tends to happen outside the mainstream and because businesses now tend to serve specific niches. With more and more individuals jumping ship to become entrepreneurs or founders, we see more diverse voices finding their audience.

TAKE CONTROL AND OVERCOME PLATEAUS

Why do I feel so passionately about personal branding? Ten years ago, I had a great job that I loved: I was Head of Communications at easyJet. It was a great company and very fulfilling six years for me.

However, following a management shake-up, I had to leave. This was gutting, but I already had an idea: I wanted to build my own communications consultancy. I was really, really excited about the idea.

But there was one big problem, and it was a global problem. The world had just come out of a recession. Plus, I had no clients, no office, no team and I could no longer rely on the clout of a well-known company to open doors for me. To top it off, I only had a few months' worth of savings to sustain myself. The clock was ticking.

How did I solve this dilemma? To draw in clients, I needed to develop my reputation. I knew a lot of relevant people, but they would not hire me unless they could see me as a credible advisor. At the time, I didn't realise that what I needed was personal branding. Only retrospectively did I come to understand the significance of taking control of my reputation.

Drawing on my skills and contacts, I worked to develop a personal brand online and offline, to establish myself as a consultant and a trusted advisor. It worked a treat and my company took off.

Over the past few years I've stepped it up a few notches after reaching a plateau. A pleasant and profitable plateau, but a plateau nonetheless.

In June 2019, my team and I had a brainstorming session to determine how we would strengthen the position of our company as one of the leading communications consultancies. My team was adamant that we should invest more in my personal brand and that it would be an asset to the company. Intellectually, I knew they were right, but I was still hesitant. They kept pushing, and I relented: "Ok, you are right, I'm 80% in. After all, I have a lot on my plate."

"No, you need to be 100% in", my colleague Lena said. I knew she was on point. "Fine, I'm all in." While already busy, I was hungry for the next level and knew from experience that enhancing my brand would give the company the necessary boost. I do not regret our decision and I am glad it wasn't a lonely decision from the top, but one we came to as a team. From publishing books to co-hosting a leading podcast, together with my team I now utilise a range of tools to reinforce my reputation as a top communications expert.

A CEO of a mobility company we interviewed on our podcast, *Speak Like a CEO*, stated that he didn't want to build a personal brand because his focus was his team. A few years ago, I had the same mindset. There is no "I" in team, right? Now, I understand that a personal brand does not subtract from the team. On the contrary, it strengthens the organisation and the team. And who says that only one person in an organisation can have a personal brand? If one person paves the way, it is easier for others to follow. Building a personal brand must never be done at the expense of the team but with the aim of empowering the team. Helping others and making them look good will only enhance your standing.

At the time of writing, we are in another recession and there are a lot of people struggling in different ways. I feel passionately about helping others who are in the same position I was in ten years ago and teaching them how to build their personal brand. My experience shows that bad things can happen at any time, but a crisis can be a great opportunity. In fact, the bigger the crisis, the bigger the opportunity.

Right now, a lot of companies are looking for new advisors and fresh ideas, and there are a lot of problems that need solving over the coming years. Personal branding allows you to position yourself as a person who solves those problems. After all, that's what business is: solving problems at scale.

PERSONAL BRANDING IS THE MOTHER OF REINVENTION

The average professional will have eleven roles in their lives. The end of lifelong employment in one company or organisation is often lamented as the end of security or as ushering in the rise of the gig economy. But let's be honest. Do we really want to go to the same office for 40 years?

I certainly don't. I started my career in Brussels, billing hours to clients from countless sectors in a hard-charging public affairs consultancy. Then, I joined General Motors' Brussels office as a lobbyist before moving back to London to join the rapidly growing, irreverent airline easyJet.

I have been fortunate that my professional experiences have been mostly positive. I have had great mentors and bosses who promoted me and treated me fairly. Still, life in a huge corporation like GM wasn't for me, neither the slow pace nor the fact that nothing could get done without consent from pretty much everyone.

My six years at easyJet were a blast. I loved it. The speed, the excitement, the knowledge that I was helping people travel and bringing Europeans closer together. The *spirit du corps* was fantastic. We were pirates, buccaneers. Traditional airlines were the regular navy – big and slow and constantly running to their governments to protect them from competition. My time at easyJet was great, until I had to reinvent myself once again. This time, it would be without a big brand, an IT helpdesk and a monthly pay-check.

All of these roles gave me insights and experiences I would not want to miss. Some were great, others less so, but all were valuable. I learnt to work in different cultures, languages and environments, with colleagues from different walks of life, from privileged graduates with their eyes on plush Brussels jobs to hard-working cabin crew members from one of England's poorest towns. I learnt about business and how to make money as an airline and how to lose it building cars. My corporate years saw 9/11, the financial crisis and the eruption of an unpronounceable Icelandic volcano. Each taught me that every crisis really is an opportunity to take risks and make changes. And most importantly, I met friends and mentors for life.

For 20 years, I've worked in different cities, countries and industries, both in-house and as a consultant. I've been a business owner since 2011. I have become a podcaster and an author. And recently, I joined the ranks of angel investors. Who knows what the next 20 years will bring?

This is my unique journey, but it is hardly atypical. Increasingly, careers now span different countries as well as periods of employment, self-employment and entrepreneurship. We spend time with our families, take sabbaticals or work from a beach for a month. I prefer the freedom and the opportunities of our current age to the monotony of the industrial age.

For those who prioritise security, there are still plenty of suitable career options, from teachers to civil servants, to lawyers and doctors. If that is your calling, that's wonderful. We need you to teach our children and heal our ailments. But when I look around, I am not sure that a stable job and a predictable career is really what makes most of us happy. Many are torn. A good friend recently told me he was feeling stuck and demotivated in his corporate career. Prestigious and secure? Yes. But fulfilling?

THE KEY TO RESILIENCE IN THE MODERN WORLD

Most of us now reinvent ourselves repeatedly throughout our working lives. For me, my career has been an adventure with many ups and downs, a journey of growth, of winning and failing forward. I never had the feeling that reinvention meant denying who I was. Rather, it was a way to discover new sides and strengths without giving up old ones.

I like to think of reinvention as coming into your own. A coming-of-age story that does not end. I have worked in cubicles, at hot desks and in my own office, in shiny buildings and smelly hangars. Now I decide where I work and with whom, partly thanks to actively caring about my brand and reputation. I have earned a level of financial freedom I would not have dreamed of ten years ago and am lucky to meet and work with people who inspire me every day. With great freedom comes great responsibility – for my team and our clients – and I try to live up to that responsibility every day.

Creating a strong personal brand can help us get unstuck. It opens new doors and brings exciting people and opportunities into our lives. A personal brand shields us from uncertainties. In the face of layoffs, global recessions or pandemics, developing your personal brand ensures that there will always be a new opportunity on the horizon. It is the key to resilience in the modern world. My hope is that this book will help you build a personal brand that is right for you. We all deserve to reach our full potential and to live happy and fulfilling lives.

CHAPTER 2

How to Make Your Mission-Driven Brand Profitable Fast

"The whole key to personal branding is to find your uniqueness so you can exploit it in the service of others." – Larry Winget, author and television personality.

What do you want to achieve in the next year? More clients? Financial freedom? To make an impact?

Opportunities arise from positive relationships with the right people. A personal brand helps you to gain the attention of people who can help take your career to the next level by speaking to the values they hold or the purposes they care about. A strong, mission-driven brand will help you help others at scale.

This approach will ensure that those people view you as a valuable partner, a trusted advisor. You will gain the reputation of a leader in your field or a go-to source of knowledge. This allows you to build a mutually beneficial relationship. As word of mouth promotes your brand, more people who need your skills and expertise will know to reach out to you.

Of course, not many people out there truly care about us. It's human nature: the vast majority of people only care when they see the value that you bring to their own lives. With this in mind, you should always try to centre your brand around the value that you bring to others. This is your purpose. Communicate your purpose clearly and the right customers will come your way.

FIVE WAYS TO MAKE YOUR PERSONAL BRAND PROFITABLE

A truly profitable personal brand puts other people first. It might seem surprising that a personal brand is not about you. It is about the people who you want to help. But by approaching your brand in this way, you will be able to expand your business and attain success. Here are five ways how:

#1 More customers will come your way.

Throughout the process of building your personal brand, you can become a trusted advisor in your field. And we all know that clients will follow you a long way if they can trust you. As your reputation as a trusted advisor increases, more potential customers will take notice. You will eventually get to the point where you can go after your dream clients instead of working on uninspiring projects or spending time chasing cold leads. As an oversubscribed business, you can pick your customers.

#2 People will be happy to pay higher prices.

The more potent your brand is, the higher the price your customers will pay for your products and services. Recognised brands can charge higher prices. Just think of how much Nike charges for shoes compared to lesser-known brands. Likewise, if you have a capacity of ten clients, but fifteen people want to work with you, you are oversubscribed. An oversubscribed business can charge more for its products and services.

#3 Get a promotion or better-paying job.

We all know that at certain stages in a career, we reach a plateau. If you work in an organisation, promotions are harder and harder to achieve the higher up you get. By investing in your brand, you are investing in your career. Before you know it, your brand will carry you far above the plateau and you will see your career reach new levels.

#4 Build a profitable business.

If you have an audience, even if it is small, it may make sense to double down on your efforts and strategically build a personal brand. This could put you in a great position to set up a new business around your audience's needs and wants. Too many businesses are only profitable because the owner works hard on it every day. If they were to leave, there would not be much of a business. A personal brand can give you the tailwind to work on the business rather than in the business. While delegating the day-to-day operations, you focus on brand building and thus grow the business and create much more value.

#5 Create multiple income streams.

On average, millionaires have seven streams of income. With a strong brand, you can also diversify your portfolio and create more sources of income. For instance, you can create products to upsell on top of your core offer. Book deals, courses, seminars, speaker gigs and many more opportunities can come your way.

I hope these five ways to increase your earnings are all the convincing you need to start the process of building your personal brand. But if you still need some convincing, I have more for you.

ATTRACTING BUSINESS, NOT CHASING IT

Chasing cold leads costs time and money. And frankly, it is exhausting and rarely results in valuable relationships. Building a successful personal brand will mean that you can spend the time you used to spend on chasing business on more fulfilling activities. Those who want to work with you will come to you, saving you time and money. Imagine the peace of mind of having customers come to you rather than worrying about winning business.

Your personal brand will also position you as the person who can answer questions in a pinch. The most valuable thing you can provide is the right advice at the right time. If you help a busy potential client once, they are likely to think of you again when they face a challenge.

And what about young professionals and recent graduates? Everything we discussed so far applies to your personal brand even if you are just starting out. Having the right universities and companies on your CV is still an asset. It opens doors for sure. But to be offered a coveted job, employers now want to see proof that graduates can actually do the job. The solution? Show your work and enhance your personal brand. This includes interactions in real life as well as a strong digital profile and a website which highlights what you are most proud of. You will already be ahead of 90% of the applicants.

What's more, I would encourage students to differentiate themselves from all the other graduates that year. For instance, I was recently interviewed by a student for the podcast of the Oxford University Media Society. When the next position opened up in my company, who do you think we hired?

Regardless of where you are in your career, a personal brand helps you provide proof of your skills and abilities before anyone asks. You will get the job over those who have not shown their skills online.

HOW TO MONETISE YOUR BRAND

A more concrete way to monetise your personal brand is to sell a product or service that aligns with your mission and purpose. Many big names sell information, either as an e-book or an online course. Think about what you have to offer; there are many more ways to profit off of your knowledge and expertise. Ultimately, you want your personal brand to enable you to make more money and to open up opportunities, not to cost you tons of time.

Personal branding consultant and author Rory Vaden came up with a framework of five business models to help you monetise your brand. Growing a following is not the same as growing an income, Rory warns. His PAIDS method will help you earn an income from the hard work you put in:

P roduct
A ds and Affiliates
I nformation
D eals
S ervices

Product: This covers any physical products you can sell. Many people who build a personal brand will offer a book on their topic of expertise. Others develop physical products that bear their names or gain recognition though their association with it.

Ads and affiliates: Your audience can be monetised if you think creatively. Building a podcast audience allows you to sell ads, for example. Affiliates are trusted partners who will pay you to promote their content, product or service to your audience. These methods allow you to monetise your personal brand without selling anything yourself.

Information: Information is the backbone of a personal brand. This includes information-based products such as books or courses delivered digitally. The global e-learning market grew to $200 billion in 2019 and continues to grow rapidly. There are plenty of opportunities to share and monetise your knowledge through creation and curation.

Since there is so much free information available online now, paid-for digital information needs to add value to your audience to be successful. If you are starting out, specifics tend to work better than high-level, general advice. Interestingly, information overload in itself is an opportunity. Audiences are willing to pay for well-curated content that saves them time and the hassle of sieving through loads of content without knowing who to trust.

Deals: This is commission-based income and includes anything that a third party pays you to do to facilitate a deal. Deals are often based on long-term contracts. Traditional book publishing or agents of any kind fall into this category. Deals may be more difficult to achieve when you are just starting out because they involve multiple parties.

Services: Services include the work of consultants and coaches, for instance. It consists of selling expertise and knowledge to those who need it. While the barrier to entry is low, it is hard to really scale the services long-term without hiring a team or automating most aspects of the process. Pairing high-quality information with implementation can be a powerful combination.

If you really want to be successful in monetising your personal brand, it is advisable to focus on one or two of the PAIDS elements. Diluted focus gets diluted results. Once you have succeeded with one or two PAIDS elements, you can consider branching out.

Once you've chosen a business model, you should make sure it will remain viable. Another helpful framework from Rory Vaden is to put all of your business ideas through the DARES test: *Is your idea digital, automated, recurring, evergreen and scalable?*

Let's take a look at what these aspects mean:

D igital
A utomated
R ecurring
E vergreen
S calable

Digital: Digital offers are enormously popular and can be accessed anywhere by anyone with an internet connection. Offering a digital product or service means that you can have a business without a physical location. This is particularly relevant as it makes your business more flexible and crisis-proof. You can offer coaching courses or design services while travelling the world or even during a global pandemic.

Automated: You do not want to have to lead your customers through every step of the buying process. You also don't want to set reminders to follow up with them, or ship product by hand. The more you can automate standard processes in your business, the more you can focus on growing the business.

Recurring: A one-off offer will only make you money once. This is clearly not scalable and is honestly not the goal of a personal brand. Make sure your offer can make you money for days, months and years to come. Acquire a customer once but keep them paying for more. Subscription services are a great way to make sure you have recurring revenue.

Evergreen: Will people be interested in your offer a month from now? How about a year from now? Make sure your product or service isn't connected to a specific event or tool that may become obsolete. Product launches will brew up excitement for your product, but they take a lot of time and energy. Aim for carrying out one big product launch that will continue to spark the interest of customers.

Scalable: You might be able to handle coaching ten clients who sign up for your service. But what about 50? You need to be able to promise the same quality no matter how many people sign up for your offer. Figure out a one-to-many business model for what you have to offer.

You won't be able to meet all five of these characteristics, as some like *recurring* and *evergreen* usually mean choosing one or the other. Choose to focus on the aspects that make most sense for your offer.

The earning potential for products or services that meet these characteristics is high. Not only will your customers remain interested and able to access your great product or service, you will also be able to continuously take on more business without having to hire a team or spend hours on end taking care of your customers.

Take a minute to think about how you could monetise your personal brand. What product or service would you offer? Does it pass the DARES test?

The simplest way to generate a scalable income from your personal brand is to focus on one business model. Adding value to the lives of your audience and potential customers will allow you to more successfully monetise your personal brand in the long run. This method will not only enable you to quickly offer a product or service that people want, it will help you maintain it for years to come.

I would encourage everyone who is aiming for financial freedom and tired of exchanging time for money to think about how to monetise your personal brand. What is your business model? What product or service would you offer? Does it pass the DARES test?

But what if you have no interest in creating products? Maybe you are a photographer, or a freelance designer. All you want is better paying clients or more compelling projects. Fortunately, there is still a way to dial up your profitability.

SAY NO TO THE HAMSTER WHEEL

We all want to see results fast when building a personal brand. But we are already busy. So how do we square this circle?

Building a personal brand is not supposed to be a second job. It is there to make our lives easier and our businesses more profitable. But input equals outcome, right? The more effort you put in, the better the results. Wrong. It is actually all about how strategic and systematic you are, not the number of hours you put in.

Zero effort equals zero results. However, many people spend a significant amount of time on their digital presence with little to show for it. They put in the effort and then give up, frustrated because they do not see the results they were hoping for. How come?

If your work is inconsistent, you won't get traction. Two hours a week one month and then nothing the next month will greatly limit your outcome. Many start highly motivated but get discouraged quickly because they don't see the results.

We see more promising results when we approach personal branding strategically. This will require some commitment each and every day, but the results are significant. By thinking strategically, you will actually save yourself time and enjoy the process. A smart approach will also ensure that your content is adding value to the lives of your audience. Keep in mind that personal branding is not about adding to the noise!

What does a strategic approach entail? It involves putting in place systems that will help you automate small tasks such as posting on social media and working from a position of clarity about your objectives and your strategy.

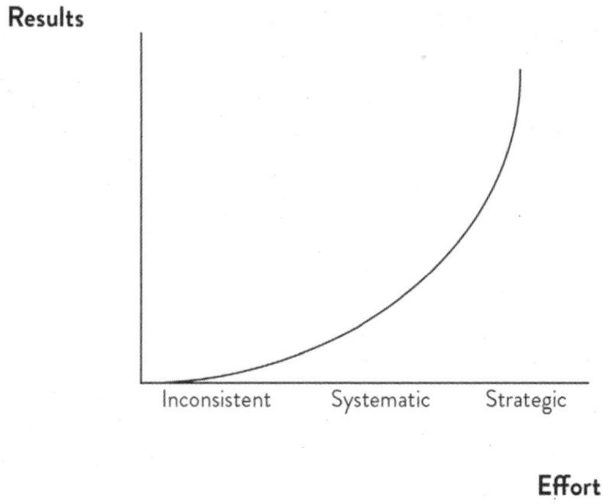

I will take you through this process in the succeeding chapters of this book. I want to show you how to approach your personal brand strategically so that you do not waste time and get discouraged.

Too many people longing to make an impact go from zero effort to inconsistent effort and then get frustrated. Or they struggle their way up to a more systematic approach over time. I believe in the opposite approach. To get it right, I start with the strategy and then put the right systems in place. This way, we are turning the usual channel-centric approach on its head.

Let's all get off the hamster wheel. Let's say yes to systems and strategies that play to our strengths and bring value to others.

Building my own brand has been an incredible source of joy, but also one of revenue. Gaining notoriety and financial freedom is attractive. But more importantly, sharing my purpose with the world has been immensely fulfilling. Ultimately, personal branding is about helping others. Solving their problems. A strong personal brand will empower you to do more of what you love for more people.

CHAPTER 3

Debunking Personal Branding Myths

"There is a way to avoid the pitfalls of self-promotion: remove the self from the promotion." – Stephen Martin and Joseph Marks, co-authors of Messengers: Who We Listen To, Who We Don't, and Why.

You want to build your brand to boost your business. You have the motivation. Who doesn't want more clients, income, freedom? But something is still holding you back.

In hundreds of conversations and trainings on the subject, a number of myths have come up frequently. Most of us have some emotional hang-ups about the subject. A nagging voice in our heads. You may think that building a brand in your name is a vanity project. Or maybe growing up you were told not to toot your own horn.

This is totally normal. Many of my friends, colleagues and peers have felt uneasy about building a personal brand. For a long time, I shared some of those concerns. However, this outlook is outdated. Don't let the world judge you or stop you from achieving your goals. Instead, tell the world who you are and what you believe in by building a strong personal brand.

CHANGE YOUR MINDSET, CREATE MOMENTUM

Everything you have heard or thought about personal branding is probably wrong. These thoughts or misgivings are futile but powerful: they shape our mindset and can hold us back from making the next move in our career. Our mindset determines how we approach building our career or business. It either helps us advance or keeps us stagnate. The good news is that we are the architect of our own mind.

Nearly all of us carry some sort of limiting belief in ourselves. In the words of brain coach Jim Kwik in his book *Limitless*, these thoughts are lies and they imprison you. Rather than remaining captive, Jim wants us to "unlimit our mindset." It's all about understanding that your potential is within your control. When you come to that understanding, the power of your potential grows dramatically.

We can grow our potential by unlearning the false assumptions we have about ourselves. If we are convinced that we can't accomplish something, we quickly reach a wall. We cannot overcome the falsehoods that we have internalised about ourselves. Jim Kwik poses this question: "So how do you minimise these limiting beliefs and develop a super-hero mindset?" He provides us with three keys:

#1 List your false assumptions.

Start paying attention each and every time you tell yourself that you are incapable of achieving something. Make a mental note.

#2 Understand the facts.

With your list of false assumptions in mind, ask yourself: do I have proof to corroborate the facts? Probably not. In reality, there is probably little hard evidence to support your false beliefs. Unfortunately, our brains are designed to worry and focus on the negative to ensure survival, not growth.

#3 Create new beliefs.

It's time to re-write history. Instead of clouding your brain with limiting beliefs, you should take the time to create new systems of thought to supplant the old ones.

Even with this knowledge, negative thoughts may still linger. Make them work for you. Susan David, a psychologist at Harvard Medical School, argues that our negative thoughts can actually help us.

In an episode of *Impact Theory* with Tom Bilyeu, Susan explains that "our emotions have evolved to help us adapt and thrive" and that there is "nothing inherently good or bad about a thought." Our thoughts and emotions simply help us navigate and understand our world. What you do with those thoughts and feelings is up to you. In other words, we should listen to our internal feedback, but not take orders from it. It is data, not direction.

Negative thoughts and emotions might not feel good, but they let us know what we care about or what points we should think through before we get started. If you are feeling uneasy about personal branding, you might be doubtful of your ability to build a successful personal brand of your own, or believe you have nothing meaningful to contribute to the debate. Most likely, we worry that we may fail or attract the disapproval of others.

Being able to listen to and learn from our negative feelings is important and powerful. From those feelings comes growth. Most people shut down when they experience these feelings and move on to more comfortable cognitive terrain. It is the successful who turn negative feelings around.

If your internal dialogue gets in your way or holds you back, I recommend you work with a coach. It can take time to shift long held beliefs, and a skilled sparring partner can be an excellent guide in this process.

Once you refuse to stay in your mental comfort zone, you can welcome any thought or feeling, positive or negative, as they may provide useful feedback. Next, analyse and consciously refute them, if they are cognitive hang-ups rather than solid reasons. Finally, use your newly gained insights to create momentum. This embodies the perfect mindset to overcome what is preventing us from reaching our full potential.

To provide an example: perhaps you have always wanted to start a podcast but have been held back by the fear that no one will listen. Take a second to analyse this fear: is it valuable? That negative feeling can actually be turned into something positive: you are afraid that no one will pay attention. That shouldn't stop you from acting, it should in fact motivate you to make a podcast that demands attention. If this is something you really want to do, you can turn that fear into drive to create a better series. This will lead to a much better end product, that has been created with a specific audience in mind.

THE EIGHT PERSONAL BRANDING MYTHS YOU SHOULD PARK ASIDE

Let's now take a look at the most commonly held false beliefs that hold individuals back. I want to help you on the journey towards getting rid of these falsehoods. Rather than wasting time on dispelling the myths mid-way through your journey to building a brand, let me set them straight right away. Let me bring the falsehoods to light, examine them with you and replace them for you.

"It's not important for me."

You may think personal branding is not for you, because in your view it isn't relevant for your job, for your field or even for your demographic. But you should not underestimate the importance of your reputation, regardless of the industry you are in. Being invisible is not a good career strategy.

For CEOs and entrepreneurs, personal reputation has a direct impact on the reputation of the business. In the CEO, Social Media and Leadership Survey by BRANDfog, 82% of respondents said they are much more likely to trust a brand when its leadership and CEO use social media. We live in a world oversaturated by products and services. It is therefore vital to take all steps necessary to ensure that potential customers perceive your brand as trusted and respectable. This allows you to become the primary choice, over all of the other, similar organisations. No visibility equals no trust.

Similarly, a 2018 survey by CareerBuilder found that 70% of employers use social media to screen candidates during the hiring process, and 43% of employers use social media to check on current employees. Your online presence is becoming as much a feature of hiring and workplace practices as in-person references from past or present colleagues and managers.

Wherever we look, reputation is becoming even more prevalent in the way that we connect with one another and the world. If you take control of your online reputation by building a strong personal brand, you maximise the chance of the right people finding and wanting to work with you.

> *New mindset: Personal branding is key to my future success. I will actively shape my reputation.*

"It won't work in my industry."

You may be of the opinion that your industry is not suited for a personal brand. You can picture countless examples of glossy personal brands encompassing marketing courses, protein shakes or shiny shoes. And your industry is simply not that glossy. However, it's your take on the industry and your personality that matter, not the industry itself.

There is an opportunity for you to break into untouched potential out there. Building a brand in a blue-collar industry means that all you say is new and unheard of. Katie Kelleher is a perfect example of a personal brand that targeted an untapped market. She is a female crane operator, and as such posts a lot about her day-to-day experiences on LinkedIn and supporting women working in construction. With her pink hair and red lipstick, Katie's posts are often more visual, prioritising videos and photos. She creates a very clear sense of her personality, offering an insight into a very unusual profession. Her audience is diverse and highly engaged because she offers a totally unique perspective on LinkedIn.

Your opinion and personality are important, and, if well presented, your audience will be excited to hear about them. Regardless of the industry you work in, you will offer a new take on the matter.

> *New mindset: Personal branding works in any industry. The fact that few people do it in my sector is an opportunity.*

"I have no time."

From emails to chores to extra projects at work, lack of sufficient time always seems to get in the way. No doubt, we are busier than ever. But busy doing what?

The average person spends 22 years of their 45-year careers in meetings, according to an MIT study. Per day, the average employee spends two-and-a-half hours on emails alone. How much of this time actually adds value to your work, your life or your career? Not much. Now add to that the amount of time that you now spend in your personal life on social media, streaming mediocre shows or scrolling through negative news. As of 2019, the average person spends 144 minutes every day on social media. That's nearly two-and-a-half hours.

Rather than filling our days with activities that are irrelevant in the great scheme of things, it pays to be intentional with our time. After all, "I have no time" is just another way of saying "It is not a priority for me." Free yourself from the priorities of others and the hundreds of distractions coming your way every day.

Instead of spending time on anxiety-inducing activities like watching the news, optimise your schedule to focus on tasks that really make a difference. Stop being a consumer and start being a producer. Skip one meeting each day or limit time spent answering emails. Once your mindset shifts, you will find that you have time for personal branding, because it brings you closer to your dream career and life.

Let me share three mind-hacks that I use all the time and that are both easy and powerful. Whenever you wonder if you should spend time on a certain task, ask yourself: Would I do this if my time was worth €1,000 per hour? If the answer is no, then eliminate, delegate, outsource, automate, or just don't do it. My time isn't worth that much, you may think. Well, if you want it to be worth €1,000 per hour, then I would encourage you to start looking at time in this way. You will be surprised how many hours are freed up all of a sudden to both build your business and be present for the people you love.

The second, similar mind-hack is called the billionaire mindset. Whenever you face a decision concerning time, ask yourself: What would a billionaire do? Probably not cleaning their own house or running errands. The billionaire mindset is also a great guide for other areas such as investing and building connections.

Finally, ask yourself what you will look back on with pride and fulfilment at the end of your professional life. No one will say, I wish I had attended more meetings, read more emails and watched more Netflix. You will be fulfilled once you have created a successful, valuable personal brand that helped you accomplish your career goals and help people.

I find these three questions incredibly powerful. They force us to become more effective and intentional with our time. Pick the mind-hack that speaks to you and apply it regularly.

This approach has allowed me to publish three books in two years, run two businesses, host a weekly podcast, serve my clients and my team, and have enough free time for hobbies, travel and a fulfilling private life. In other words, I make my priorities my priorities. Personal branding is part of that, because it is key to professional success. Conversely, not finding time to build a personal brand is very costly.

Rather than looking at time spent, look at the return on your time invested and on the costs of not being visible.

I have therefore long ceased to use the phrase "I don't have time." Activities are either a priority or they are not.

> *New mindset: I am in control of my time. I will prioritise the life-changing activities that bring me closer to my goals.*

"I need a charismatic magnetic personality."

Personal branding in business is not about chasing followers. It is not about good looks or becoming a larger-than-life character. Your goal is to become a thought-leader and to attract the attention of those who matter to you, those who you want to help with your knowledge or expertise. If your content aligns with what you want to accomplish with your business, you will gain traction online and offline. Besides, charisma correlates strongly with leadership. If you work towards becoming a thought-leader, your audience will perceive you as more charismatic.

A thought-leader is dynamic and energetic. That's why it is so important to optimise your personal branding strategy for energy. Like time, energy is under your control with the right systems and mind-hacks. In chapter five, we will cover how to protect and maximise energy.

> *New mindset: I have the personality to create an authentic personal brand. My energy will propel my brand forward.*

"I don't have anything to say."

Not true. If you have a business or a career, you really have something to say of value to your audience. In the next section, I share some ideas on how to generate content in a time-efficient manner that upholds your personal brand.

In addition, by focusing on your skills and knowledge, you will come across as genuine. At times, personal brands that rely simply on a charismatic personality suffer from inauthenticity. If they fail to be useful to others, they quickly become irrelevant when a new person with a more interesting personality arrives on the scene. At some point, those personalities will run out of things to say and will lose the attention of the audience. Your personal brand, on the other hand, should add value and it will continue to gain the attention of those who matter.

If you still feel unsure, enlist the help of a sparring partner. We all have a friend with whom we have great, inspiring conversations. Exchange ideas related to your field. Make sure to record your session so you can come back to it and reassure yourself that you really do have something to say.

Do you consider yourself an introvert? This may be a secret power, not a hinderance. You tend to think before you speak (or write). You have truly insightful things to say that extroverts may not think of. Your personal brand gives you a platform to share these innovative ideas without being shot down by a louder colleague during a meeting.

New mindset: My skills and knowledge matter to my audience. They will pay attention.

"Social media is a waste of time and not important."

I agree that there are many things about social media that limit its appeal. But I am not suggesting that you are a mindless consumer of content or partake in the outrage machine. Nor that you try to play the volume-game of trying to grow on all platforms at the same time. This will only lead you to burn-out.

Instead, think of social media strategically. You are not adding to the noise, you are increasing your visibility. From a business perspective, social media channels are free tools that are at your disposal. In Part II, we will develop your personal strategy for social media that takes account of your objectives and preferences and thus maximises results. With a targeted approach and positive results, I wager a guess that you will grow to like what social networks can do for you and your business.

> *New mindset: Social media channels are useful tools for my business, if used strategically.*

"I can't put something out unless it is perfect."

Personal brands are built on progress, not perfection. Perfection is not relatable nor credible, so aiming for it is not just futile but actually counterproductive.

Whenever I think "It's not good enough or I am not good at this", I quickly add the word *yet*. This turns my mindset around in a split second. I simply do the best I can at that moment, test it and pivot it, if necessary. In this way, I move from my comfort zone to my growth zone. Yesterday's growth zone quickly becomes a comfort zone, and a huge step forward has been made. In this way, you can enter a virtuous circle of permanent growth.

New mindset: I get things done and improve over time. The more I create, the better and faster I will get.

"It's not about me, it's about the team."

Personal branding is not just about gaining notoriety amongst an external audience. Internal audiences – your employees – can also benefit greatly from a well-thought-out personal brand. Your company will benefit greatly from hiring employees who are excited and motivated to work with you.

Aiga Senftleben, co-founder of the fintech company Billie was recently named one of Sifted's fifteen women in European tech to watch. On personal branding, Aiga says: "I realised it is very good for employees. Women who work here come up to me and say, 'I feel that because you are there, I can be there too'... If you want to have a diverse company, you need to have a diverse workforce."

Similarly, your role model mindset will ensure that your personal brand will enhance and empower the team.

New mindset: I will use my personal brand to strengthen the team and the business.

Before you move on, make sure you reconcile any lingering hang-ups you may have.

AVOID THESE SIX COMMON MISTAKES

You're now fully on the way to creating a powerful, profitable personal brand. You have parked the resistant mindset away. You understand that your brand centres around the needs of others, that it can help you make a big change in your life and that you do have enough to say online. I know you are eager to get started, but I want to give you some pointers on what to avoid with your personal brand. So many of the personal branding guides out there focus on the do's, so it is really important – and helpful to you – to understand what makes a brand fail, and how you can avoid the same fate.

There are six common mistakes that people make when building a personal brand. I mention these mistakes throughout this book, but they are so vital to the success of a personal brand that I want to put them all in a single subsection for easy reference.

#1 Don't mix brand and sales.

You might be thinking that this can't be true because so many famous people use their personal brands to sell things. However, they did not build their brand by selling straight away. They built their personal brand by providing entertainment, value or insights. Only after they gained some success did they begin to sell.

No one likes a hard seller. If you do decide to mix in some sales messaging, make sure it is only a small portion of your overall content. For instance, one out of eight posts should be about sales. You should clearly distinguish between value-adding content and sales posts. People are not keen on sneaky, back-door sales tricks. However, if you're upfront and only do it from time to time, your audience will not be put off. Keep in mind: everyone wants to be helped, no one wants to be sold to.

#2 Don't make it about yourself.

If what you are producing is seen as a vanity project, people will not respond to it. Even celebrities go to great lengths to stress that they are doing it for their fans. And those who get high on their own supply often face a rude awakening when their fans are turned off by their selfish antics.

Besides, in the business world, a personal brand must be about value for your clients, for your customers, for your audiences and for your community. That's what it's all about. By definition, your personal brand will not be a vanity project if you make it about others.

#3 Don't fake it.

Being authentic means that there's alignment between what you say, what you do and who you are.

Let's say an inauthentic person is actually successful building a personal brand. What have they achieved in doing so? Not much of value. An inauthentic brand attracts the wrong audience. If you instead build an authentic brand, you will be successful quicker because you are attracting the attention of people and opportunities that will actually help you achieve your goals.

#4 Don't be vanilla.

There is so much bland content out there already. You know it when you spot it. We all have opinions. Don't be afraid to share yours. This is not a suggestion to be polarising. Your goal is not to sew disunion. However, you should express your opinion in a way that encourages discussion. You're not reporting the news in a balanced way. You are expressing your opinion or expert take on a subject matter that you have a lot of experience with and knowledge of. You need to stand for something.

#5 If you confuse, you lose.

When building a personal brand, you may feel pressured to put out a lot of content. That pressure often drives some people to create content in a rush. That content tends to be random and confusing. As Donald Miller, CEO of marketing company StoryBrand argues, "if you confuse, you lose." Your audience needs to be able to immediately understand your narrative. Be clear about what you want to be known for. Make sure to create systems that will help you stay on message.

#6 Don't lose pace.

Building and maintaining a successful personal brand takes time. There are ways to make it more systematic and efficient, but it does take time. A lot of people get frustrated during the process and give up, only to start again at some other point. This start-and-stop approach leads to inconsistency. If we don't commit to putting in the necessary effort, we will simply be unable to build a personal brand. This is a marathon, not a sprint. Personal brands need to be constantly given attention.

If you avoid these six common mistakes, you will build a personal brand that continues to deliver value-adding content that your audience will love. Be the person online that you truly are and you will find an audience that trusts you. In the next section, I will show you how to execute your personal brand. When building your strategy and thinking about your tactics in the next section, check back and make sure the tools you have chosen will help you avoid these six mistakes.

MOTIVATION, MINDSET, METHOD AND MESSAGE

You now understand why creating a personal branding is beneficial and profitable. You are motivated, and you have adapted your mindset and addressed any major concerns. As Jim Kwik points out in his book *Limitless*, with motivation, mindset and method in check, you are on the journey to realise your fullest potential.

I added another aspect to this framework – message. I call this framework the "4 M's" to help you keep in mind the most important aspects of a successful personal brand. The Venn diagram at the beginning of Part I will help you visualise these aspects. Later on, I explain in more detail the power of a good message.

Before I introduce you to *how* you can go about building your successful personal brand, I want you to take a moment to think about what this journey means for you. Write down what you will gain by building a personal brand and what you will avoid. Come back to this personal analysis whenever you need a boost of motivation or feel doubts creeping in.

Motivation isn't a tangible thing that is out there somewhere waiting to be found. Motivation has to be built. And that is why exercises such as the above are so important at this stage of your journey. Ninety percent of the options and advice you have probably already encountered do not fit with your personal needs and goals. That is why I stress the importance of honestly tailoring your personal brand to your values, your purpose, your goals. Only by being true to yourself can you build lasting motivation.

You should now feel at ease about the journey that lies ahead of you. It is a journey that takes 30 days, but also one that lasts forever. This journey will allow you to become a magnet to those who matter to you. Becoming unignorable is key to your success and I am here with you every step of the way. I went through the same steps as you did. Ten years ago, I was unconvinced of the true value of building a personal brand. Had I understood the potential of a personal brand, I would have started earlier. It is my mission now to help you build and benefit from a personal brand.

PART II

BUILD YOUR BRAND IN 30 DAYS

In Part I, you laid the groundwork to become a magnet to those who matter to you and your business. A personal brand can help you achieve your goals. To get started, you have to find your motivation and adopt the right mindset. We have to ask ourselves why. To really succeed at building a personal brand, you have to want it. You have to commit to it.

In Part II, I take you through the process of building your personal brand in just 30 days. I will walk you through the steps needed, and I would encourage you to schedule and actually carry out these tasks within this timeframe. It is entirely doable! Block time out in your calendar for each step and you will have all the time you need to build a successful personal brand.

This 30-day framework is actually flexible based on your ambition and personal situation. It works well for those who work full-time or have family obligations. For some, 30 days may be far too long. For others, 30 days may not be enough time to thoroughly think through a successful personal brand strategy. Do what works for you, but keep up the momentum! If you already have a clear idea of why you want to build a personal brand, you may only need a weekend or two to complete this journey.

Others might need more time. If you are unclear about your "why", take some time to talk to others to help you find your motivators. There are many resources out there to help you in this process. Professional coaches, seminars or even online communities can assist you. Clarity is key, so do not be afraid to add some extra time to this journey.

The first step is to achieve clarity on why you are building your personal brand and what you want to accomplish with it. Next, I lead you through drafting your strategy and choosing the tactics that are right for you. The final phase consists of guidance on how to execute your strategy and get started on your personal branding journey.

By the end of these 30 days (more or less), you should have a clear brand and strategy and understand how to quickly achieve positive results. In week one, you will already see the first valuable outcomes and quick wins.

At each step along your journey, keep track of your progress. You can download the accompanying *Unignorable Workbook* at oliveraust.com/unignorable. It contains exercises to guide and motivate you.

At the end of the 30 days, you will have created the foundations of a sustainable brand that puts you on the path to become truly unignorable. These four weeks will teach you how to develop and build upon your personal brand in case your goals or career change. You will be equipped with the right method to make sure your personal brand is effective in every new situation.

CHAPTER 4

Achieve Clarity

"Next to doing the right thing, the most important thing is to let people know you are doing the right thing." – John D. Rockefeller, business magnate and philanthropist.

In 30 days or less, you can completely change the way that people perceive you. It is a method I have used with clients many times before. And with this new reputation, you make yourself resilient to the challenges that might come your way.

In this section, you will learn how to build a personal branding strategy that results in the reputation that you want to have. Make sure your reputation is a true reflection of your goals and you will see progress more quickly than you could have imagined.

I like to outline this journey in the following steps:

Week one: Achieve clarity. Find your north star and make it the basis of your brand.

Week two: Formulate your strategy. Your strategy is your overall approach that will tie all of your efforts together.

Week three: Choose your tactics. These are the tools that you will use on a daily basis to push your brand forward.

Week four: Build a system to execute your plan with impact. As long as you complete one step per week, you can build your brand in just one month. Blocking half a day per week tends to be sufficient and works well for those who work full time or have a family.

You can also move slower or faster, for instance by blocking one weekend to complete four steps. If you are highly productive and motivated, this may work for you.

My team and I have built a community of like-minded professionals who are completing their own personal branding journeys. Each member of this online community has taken part in one of our bootcamps, in which we build your personal brand together. Check out oliveraust.com for more details on our bootcamp and to join our community. In addition to benefiting from the collective experience of my team and I, you can lean on a community of people who have been on the same journey and who can answer your questions.

Now, let's get started!

KNOW YOUR WHY

For the first week, you are going to nail down exactly why you want to build a personal brand, what you want to gain from it and who you would like your personal brand to appeal to. In our lives and in our careers, it is hard enough to achieve what we set out to. Without clarity, it is very unlikely that we will reach our full potential. The exercises in this section are designed to cut through your current thought-processes and reach the core of your intentions. In doing so, they will be your north star as you build your brand.

So why are you putting effort into building a personal brand? Once you figure out the reason, you will be able to focus on creating a personal brand that reflects your goals. You need to know what fulfils you in order to immerse yourself fully in your brand. It is best to iron out your "why" before moving on to the next steps in your personal brand journey. This may take a few hours, a week or longer. No matter how much time you need, make sure you're are crystal clear in your reasoning before you start the next steps.

The following exercise is called the *five whys* and was developed by Sakichi Toyoda during the evolution of Toyota's manufacturing methodologies. The intention is to get to the bottom of your deepest desires and motivations. This exercise is incredibly enlightening, especially if you complete it with another person. As with most self-reflection exercises, the input of a trusted friend or coach can push us to discover something new about ourselves.

I recently asked a friend to do the exercise. This is the result:

"Why do you want to create a personal brand?"

"I want to take the next step in my career."

"Why do you want to take the next step in your career?"

"I want financial security."

"Why do you want financial security?"

"So I can spend more time with my family."

Up until this point, his motivation was clear to himself. He became reluctant, but I kept asking.

"Why do you want to spend more time with your family?"

"Because I want to be a good husband and father."

This is where it got really emotional.

"Why do you want to be a good husband and father?"

"Because my father never was."

Our most powerful *why* is usually tied to our identity. My friend wants to be a good father and husband; that is part of the core of his being. He does not want his family to have financial worries and he wants them to be secure so they can spend time together.

It is crucial for him to understand his real *why*, because the first, superficial answer may have led him astray. In fact, it has led him astray before. He once made a career move which required a long commute, meaning less time with his family. This did not make him happy.

Finding out his true *why* has huge implications for his personal branding strategy. For him, it is not about becoming a CEO or a big-time business owner. It is about having choice in his career. Being seen as so good that future employers or clients can't ignore you, meaning he will have more control over his working life.

You can carry out the exercise for yourself but working with a coach tends to be more effective. Working with a coach, friend or colleague will also help keep you on track. It will also give you a sparring partner to creatively and effectively develop ideas if you are feeling unsure. The real answers are often hidden underneath, and we may require a push from a well-meaning person to get closer to the truth. In any case, make sure to record your responses for future reference.

EYES ON THE PRIZE

Based on the exercise that you have just completed, I suggest you write down the things that you would like to achieve professionally. What are your big dreams? Do you want to be financially independent? Leave a legacy? Make an impact? The final "why" that you wrote down in the last exercise is a hint at the big dreams that you have.

Keep your eyes on this prize. Your personal brand will help you get there, day by day. No one will achieve all their dreams in a month or a year. But your personal brand can become a vehicle to increase your visibility, to help you help thousands of others.

What's the harm in dreaming big? If you fail, you will at least accomplish bigger goals than you would have if you stayed within your comfort zone. Dreaming big also encourages creative thinking which in turn leads to bigger results. You are on your way to becoming unignorable, and the unignorable pursue big ambitions.

On the path to reaching your long-term goals, there may be some smaller, quicker wins. Such goals could include how many clients you would like to win, any dream clients you would like to add to your portfolio, financial goals that you would like to hit, perhaps even speaking engagements or events that you would like to run. These smaller goals will help you reach your big dreams. This exercise is designed to paint a picture of the professional experiences that you would like to have in one year's time. Vague goals get vague results, so be as specific as you can be.

Here are some examples:

- I want so many new clients that I become oversubscribed
- I want to win five dream clients
- I want to increase my revenue
- I want to give a TEDx talk
- I no longer want to pursue cold leads

With this picture, you now need to take a moment to consider *how* exactly you would like a personal brand to contribute to this.

The intention is to think about all of the different ways that a personal brand will direct you towards your goal. This will help you to be more creative with your brand and ensure that what you do online is part of a wider strategy.

Clarity is the most valuable tool that you have when building a personal brand and developing your strategy. Once you have completed these two exercises for yourself, you can pinpoint exactly what you want to achieve and why you want to achieve it.

BE CLEAR ABOUT YOUR VALUES

Purpose-driven organisations have become a major trend over the course of the last decade. With more options than ever before, customers have much more scope to buy from or partner with the brands that align with their values. This has driven a seismic shift in the world of business. Marketing in particular focuses as much around the values of the company as it does around the products or services they provide. I outlined how this can make your personal brand profitable in the previous section. Here, I provide you with some tools to help you clarify your purpose.

Brands can be categorised in two ways: belief brands and promise brands. Promise brands make promises in order to sell products. For example, "this shampoo will give you beautiful hair." Belief brands ask their customers to buy into a belief system before introducing the products. For example, disruptor brands like Oatly have gained dedicated followings by articulating their beliefs in everything that they do. The oat milk manufacturer lays out its beliefs on its website: "Our sole purpose as a company is to make it easy for people to turn what they eat and drink into personal moments of healthy joy without recklessly taxing the planet's resources in the process." In the past few years, this has won them many, many hearts. The Swedish company has earned investments from celebrities such as Oprah, Natalie Portman and Jay-Z. Meanwhile, many of the traditional brands are losing support as a result of their failure or unwillingness to transition to more purpose-driven practices.

The effects of this change in the consumer world have started to seep into the way that individuals consume content and information. Many people seek to follow those individuals online that view the world from a relatable perspective. When building a personal brand, it is important to centre your values in the way that you behave and communicate. The result is that you build an audience who understands that purpose. They are more receptive to your ideas and even your products, because they are confident it is coming from someone who shares their world view, someone working towards a common vision.

Values are appealing when they focus on others. Mathis Büchi founded the tax filing app Taxfix four years ago with a clear mission. He set out to help people get their money back. His customers were top-of-mind: he identified the hassle of going through tax returns and made it simple for the average citizen. What's more, he has fostered a positive company culture within his own start-up. Recently, he announced

Taxfix employees who have been part of the company since its early days could sell off their share options. A total of €3.8 million was paid out to employees who had contributed to the company's growth. Mathis was eager to compensate early employees who took the risk of joining an early-stage start-up. With this move, he demonstrated that he deeply cares about his team.

Finally, Mathis stands up for what is right. After receiving a letter from a user who complained about the use of a person of colour in Taxfix's ads, Mathis decided to publish the letter online. The blatant racism of the letter disgusted the founder, who took a clear stand on the matter. His LinkedIn post was clear: "I am posting this because it's easy to forget in our bubble how very real racism still is and that every one of us must act to bring an end to it", he wrote. Taken together, these actions give Taxfix customers a clear idea of what the company stands for.

You will already, I'm sure, have a clear idea of your values. They are ingrained in you and will already affect the decisions that you take on a daily basis. Now I will ask you to write down your three most important values. Moving forward through the next few weeks, ask yourself regularly whether the choices that you are making fit into this core set of beliefs. Even if you never explicitly state the values online, they will be obvious in the way that you behave and the things that you say.

Are you stuck on what your values are? Sit down with a close friend and have a chat about what you care about. Your friend will have a good idea if these values are authentic to you. Chatting with a friend is a great way to get unstuck.

DEFINE YOUR BRAND

The final element of this first week – finding clarity – is to define your brand identity. What is the ONE thing that you want to be known for? In other words, what does your brand stand for? If there is one thing your audience should remember about you, what would it be?

We all have complex personalities and multiple interests and talents. We will get to those shortly. For now, our goal is to gain clarity about what you want to be synonymous with. In which specific area do you want to be a thought-leader? Once you have chosen the one thing you want to be known for, make sure it is at the centre of your brand identity. If you confuse, you lose.

The reason is that it is very hard to be known for several things when you are building your brand. Interestingly, once you are known for one thing, it gets easier to establish yourself in a related field. Once we trust a person as an expert in one area, we are more likely to trust them in other fields as well. This is called the "halo effect". In short, become known for one thing and only then branch out if you desire.

The next step is to define your personal brand pillars. These are three to five topics that make you who you are and give you your unique personality. They need to be genuine, and you need to be comfortable talking about them in public. You alone decide where you draw the line between the personal and the private.

Let's take Dr Sophie Chung, founder and CEO of Qunomedical, as an example.

Startup Life	Fitness
Motherhood	Female Entrepreneurship

These four pillars make Sophie who she is, while keeping her content focused on a few key areas. The four elements complement each other and therefore enhance her standing as a well-known founder of a successful healthcare start-up. If she would limit what she shares to healthcare and start-ups, her appeal would be limited to this audience. By including topics that a wider audience can relate to, she significantly broadened her appeal. Her 22,000 followers on Instagram certainly think so.

What if you have two professional interests that have nothing to do with each other?

Think about Peter Garrett, the lead singer of the Australian rock band Midnight Oil. He was able to combine his passion for music with his commitment to the environment, taking office in the Australian House of Representatives. His two passion projects merged into one when he was appointed Minister for Environment Protection, Heritage and the Arts in 2010.

Fortunately, we do not expect anyone to fit into a neat professional box anymore. And being a musician in addition to running for office makes Peter Garrett unique and interesting. It sets him apart and makes him more remarkable than others who only have one of these skills. Note however, that he was a musician first, and then a politician. He did not try to launch both careers simultaneously.

It can get confusing for your audience when you are in the middle of a career change or are building a business in addition to your day job. If those careers are unrelated, it makes sense to focus on what is most important to your future and build your audience there. If your future and your current career are related, you could develop a reputation as a trusted expert in your industry, regardless of your current position.

An authentic, successful brand will highlight what makes you different. Derek Sivers, a well-known American entrepreneur, tells us that deeper branding focuses on what sets you apart from others. Reflect on your quirks in every aspect of your personal brand, from your website to how you interact with potential clients and customers.

What can we learn from deep branding? Don't be afraid to put your true self out there. Your audience will appreciate it and connect even more deeply with you and your brand.

Define your own personal branding pillars and keep them on your desk to make sure your personal brand is clear and focused.

Now that you are clear on your *why*, what you stand for and your brand identity, let's move onto your audience. Heart and soul allow people to see the things that make you tick. If they feel the same, you develop an affinity even through a screen.

In his bestselling guide *Building a Story Brand*, marketing expert Donald Miller argues that expressing empathy will build trust and foster a relationship with your audience. However, authority is needed to position yourself as a trusted expert. Your customers or clients do not want a sounding board to complain to and offer no response in return. They want someone who will listen and then solve their problems. This also falls in line with the basic business concept of "know me, like me, trust me, pay me". Building relationships with potential customers is great, but you need trust to convert that relationship into sales.

IDENTIFY YOUR AUDIENCE

Kevin Kelly's famous blog post, *1,000 true fans*, outlines the idea that 1,000 people who will spend $100 on you every year is all you need for a comfortable life. Building an audience of highly engaged supporters is infinitely more fruitful than a million disengaged connections.

It is important to gain clarity on who you actually want to reach now that you have gained clarity on your personal brand. Doing so will allow you to tailor every post and every interaction to building a strong connection with those select few that make up your audience. Who do you want to talk to? Who do you need to convince of your skills and abilities? Where can you find these people online? Answering these questions is vital to the success of your personal brand.

Take Patreon. They seek to help all the creatives out there – podcasters, artists, musicians, video creators – to build direct relationships with their most engaged fans. By using the Patreon platform, creatives can engage directly with their audiences, be it through loyalty discounts, group chats, member-only shows, polls, early updates or public shoutouts. With Patreon, creatives can enjoy healthier, kinder and meaningful interactions with their fan base.

Take some time to think about the demographics (who they are) and psychographics (what they think and feel) of your ideal audience. This will impact where and how you communicate. Demographics include gender, age, education, location and nationality. Psychographics are characteristics related to psychology and include interests, values and concerns. Both are equally important in gaining a full understanding of your target audience.

Who your audience is will also impact what you say on the various platforms you choose. What questions do they need answered? Think about the specific advice your audience needs in the moment. Your content should reflect that. There is a lot of general, evergreen advice on the internet. That content is useful, but there is definitely an information glut that makes it hard to stand out. Instead, ask some of your current clients or customers what pain points they are experiencing and base your content around that.

Remember, it's about who you reach, not how many people you reach. Seth Godin, the marketing guru, emphasises the value of the "minimum viable audience". If your audience is everyone, you have to dumb down your content and make it appeal to the average person. This made sense in the days when there were a few TV networks and tabloid newspapers. Today, in our multi-media environment, it is a recipe for failure. If you try to be everything to everybody, you end up being nothing to no one.

Instead, try to gain the attention of those who really matter. Go after the smallest market that is viable to you and your business. That audience will, in the end, mean more for you because they will actually pay attention to what you have to say and will be more interested in buying your product or service. Even more, they will tell others about you. Once you have an engaged network of 1,000 true fans, you have the perfect basis to grow your audience if you chose to do so.

Again, this is where a professional coach or trusted peer can be of immense help. It can be difficult to differentiate for yourself between your *ideal* audience and your *actual* audience. Perhaps you want the attention of high-level CEOs but are attracting the attention of young professionals. Talking to someone who is outside of your business can help give you perspective.

Seth Godin also makes the point that by focusing on your minimum viable audience, you will cut through the noise of endless content that is available online. He says: "If it's not relevant, it's noise. If it's untrusted, unwelcome or selfish, it's noise. But your contribution isn't noise. Not for the right people, at the right time."

I want to lead you through a short exercise that will help you hone in on how you can make sure you are adding value to those who matter.

I call this the "top ten" exercise. Think about the questions below based on your audience demographics and psychographics.

- Who are the top ten people that will make the biggest difference to your journey?
- Talk to them and learn how you can provide them value. What are their pain-points? How can you help?

Once you have answered these questions, you will be able to create content that is valuable to your top ten. Your aim is to be famous for the few, not the many. Later on, you can expand this list to your Dream 100 targets.

To recap, in order to build a successful brand, it is important to be clear on four main points: your why, your brand identity, your audience and the problem you solve. If you ever find yourself getting lost or uncertain, come back to these points. They will always keep you on the right track.

It's the end of week one, the first step in your personal branding journey. Now that you have gained clarity on your personal brand and defined your audience, we can dive into developing your strategy. In the next section, I give you some guidance and examples to help you develop your own personal branding strategy. My aim is not to give you a standard solution, but to prompt you to create a strategy that is tailor-made to help you achieve your goals.

CHAPTER 5

Formulate Your Strategy

"Success is no longer related to the volume of tasks you complete but rather the significance of them." – Rory Vaden, personal branding expert.

The downfall of most personal branding guides or courses is that they focus too much on a "one-size-fits-all" solution. Someone is successful, deconstructs their success and then tells the world: this is the method you should follow. You listen to a few of them and get confused by all the conflicting advice. A second frequent shortcoming is a focus on granular, ever-changing channel tactics. After all, you want to build a personal brand to boost your business or career, not become a channel manager.

I want *you* to succeed. What's more, I want you to succeed your way. The way to achieve this is to develop a personal branding strategy that works for you – not against you. My approach centres on your strategies and tactics, helping you develop your own systems rather than trying to shoehorn your voice into a framework that was designed for someone else.

This is about using the tools available in a way that is authentic to you. I want to give you the means to tailor-make your own strategy. And these skills are evergreen – tools and channels might change, but the lessons you learn in this section will allow you to develop your personal brand at any stage of your life and career.

Play to your strengths, be personal and be yourself.

STRATEGY IS HOW YOU PLAN TO ACHIEVE YOUR GOALS

This is the second week of your 30-day journey, or the second step if you condense it into one weekend or expand it to a few weeks. Remember, do what works for you and your lifestyle! Building on the brand identity statements that you wrote in the last chapter, this section helps you develop your identity into a brand narrative that others can engage with. To help you tell your story in a compelling way, I give you the ultimate formula for writing your personal statement. In the final part of this chapter, you will learn how to formulate your key messaging, to ensure that your content is geared towards the audience that you envisioned in the previous section.

Think of the two prominent digital marketers of recent years: Gary Vaynerchuk and Melanie Deziel. Both have very different personal brands, but each fit their personalities and aims.

Gary Vaynerchuk is loud, he is in-your-face. He also has a huge team of people just producing content about his daily whereabouts. He's firing on all cylinders. Gary Vee thrives on the visual. He is not a writer and by his own admission, he's not a reader either. The content he produces typically features him speaking on subjects that are important to him. One of those topics is digital marketing. He regularly shares his life, his thoughts and his story with his audience.

Now, look at Melanie. Melanie Deziel is discreet but powerful. As the founder and Chief Content Officer of StoryFuel, she is a leader in her field. Despite her international success and many awards, she remains grounded and down-to-earth. Her tone is personal, yet more professional than Gary's. Her social media presence alternates between family pictures, lifestyle content and book recommendations. Her blog serves as her expert-voice and features little to no personal content.

These are two very different approaches. But these are also two very different people. The approaches that Gary and Melanie choose are informed by their personalities. They are choosing the method that works for them. I am not saying you should do exactly as these two do, but that you should focus on an approach that suits you. Do it your way, not the way that you see others doing it. You can always take inspiration from others. Every choice you make, however, should feel like a natural action. If it feels forced, it will come across as inauthentic.

Focusing on methods that fit you will also make your personal brand sustainable. If you chose tactics that you dread, say videos, then maintaining your personal brand will be hard work. Instead, by focusing on things that you actually like, working on your personal brand will not be a chore. It may even be fun!

One important caveat: we all tend to be uncomfortable with new channels or tools. This does not mean we should dismiss them, if they might be useful for enhancing our reputation. No one is great shooting videos or speaking in public unless they practice it consistently. But there are certainly some channels that are not our preference for a variety of reasons. For instance, I have used Twitter professionally for over a decade and can safely say that it is not my favourite channel. Conversely, I was sceptical about Instagram when it emerged but have grown to like it after using it because it is more positive and playful than Twitter. When you have these realisations about different channels, listen to them. Otherwise you will end up dreading the process.

MAXIMISE FOR ENERGY

This approach will also help you come across as authentic, engaged and interesting. You will be able to maximise your passion and sustain your energy.

I can't stress enough how important energy is in the context of creating your brand. Without maximising for energy, it is impossible to stay motivated in the long run. We have all started projects with the best of intentions and abandoned it after a few weeks of hard graft because it no longer excited us. So how do you keep energy levels up?

The key is to be intentional and mindful about your approach to personal branding. Not long ago, I realised that speaking *with* people gives me energy whilst speaking *at* people drains me of my energy. Human interaction is my fuel. That's why I love running workshops, podcasts and bootcamps and try to avoid one-way communication like webinars.

When it comes to the podcast *Speak Like a CEO*, which I co-host with my colleague Lena Carlson, we truly enjoy the conversations with the founders, CEOs and experts we interview. We build our brand while discussing topics we are passionate about with truly accomplished people. It feels like a privilege, not a chore.

There is no point in becoming great at doing the wrong thing, or worse, at something you hate. It will suck the energy out of you. When you develop your strategy and then pick your tactics, ask yourself: will this approach energise or tire you? Approaching personal branding with a long-term view also means pacing yourself. Pick the tools that you find energising and do them incredibly well week in, week out. Don't try to do everything at once, or you'll quickly find that the balancing act is too much.

DECIDE ON YOUR APPROACH

Do you pursue your goals alone, in a team or in collaboration with others? Your approach to personal branding must be informed, developed and executed by you. It can be enhanced by collaborating with others with complimentary skills or ideas.

If you are at an early stage of your career and work without a team or have a limited network, you will want to prioritise the tools and channels that can have impact without the input from others. If you lead a company or have a team whose skills you can borrow, this will offer up more options as you devise your strategy. For example, if you work with a great graphic designer, ask for support on visual content generation.

During this second step, start to think about the people within your current professional network. If there are others with complimentary skills, there is potential for some interesting, mutually beneficial relationships to arise from brand building.

Tijen Onaran, a public speaker, writer and moderator, founded the group Global Digital Women, in order to develop a network of women who work in digitalisation. Her personal brand centres around the development and purpose of this network, meaning the majority of her content focuses on the work of other people. Doing so allows Tijen to produce engaging, high-quality content that brings a broad range of perspectives to her audience and gives her credibility as well.

Including other professionals in your own personal branding activities broadens your capabilities and also allows you to widen your audience. A collaborative approach is also self-reinforcing: your personal brand will grow as your network grows, and your network will grow as you begin to work with new people. This is also one of the most exciting aspects of personal branding activities. Meeting new collaborators encourages you to think in new ways and learn new skills from those around you.

For now, simply decide on whether you decide to do it on your own, or with a team.

YOUR POSITIONING

When building an audience, it is very important that people understand the value that you can bring to their lives. We all have something to add, and successful professionals are very good at framing their talents in a way that centres around other people. What are the most important attributes that people should know about your work? Answer the following sentences for yourself: "I…" and "I help…to…".

The first sentence is concerned with your skills or your unique selling point. Your second statement is more focused on your purpose, your priorities in life, the way that you want to change the world.

When completing these statements, I answer: "I am on a mission to ensuring others reach their full potential. I help high-profile individuals and organisations to take their reputation to the next level so they can build future-proof businesses." In the first sentence, I talk about my passion. In the second, I focus on my professional outlook in relation to others.

I completed this task with my team, and this is how some of them responded:

"I am the person who makes other people sound amazing. I help business-minded or technical individuals share their ideas in a compelling way." (Head of Audio Production)

"I am the person with an eye for visuals. I help clients tell their stories with beautiful design and videos." (Head of Design)

"I am the person who designs digital campaigns. I help clients to break out of the box and think in new ways." (Senior Account Manager)

As you can see, this exercise is designed to fit your work and your skills. It enables you to present those skills as valuable attributes for other people in a simple and understandable way.

The most successful brands tap into others' fundamental truths. If you can find a way to add value to your audience's lives, they will keep on coming back. They will see that you are enriching their day-to-day reality and their future success.

We all bring something valuable to the table. Everyone has skills and characteristics that they can offer to help others in some way. Some obvious examples are doctors, lawyers and plumbers. But successful people in *any* profession are successful because they add value and solve problems.

There *is* something about you that makes you extremely valuable. This should be the centre of your brand.

HOW DO I WRITE ABOUT MYSELF?

Now that you know how to frame your skills in a way that is relevant to others, the next task for week two is to expand upon this and create a brand statement. Brand statements lay out your intentions, values and skills in a compelling narrative. For traditional big brands, this brand statement might be found on their company website or it might be an internal document that constantly informs strategic decisions the company makes. For a personal brand it is effectively your LinkedIn bio, the "About Me" text on your website or the prose at the top of your CV.

Writing about yourself has become an essential skill in the modern, digital world. These days, thanks to social media, we have the opportunity to write about ourselves much more often. And the consequence of this is that companies and clients no longer just look at your achievements to make hiring decisions. People want to work with individuals that reflect their values.

Approach writing about yourself as an opportunity to highlight your personality, your interests and your passions. You are aiming to build a picture of the person *behind* the accomplishments. If you treat it this way, this process can be a great way to get to know yourself better.

Remember that no matter what you say, people will only remember one key message in a piece of text. This is perhaps the most valuable piece of writing advice around. The best writers decide what that message will be from the start and weave it throughout the text to ensure the audience remembers the right thing.

To find your key message, go back to the two sentences, "I..." and "I help...to...". Your key message will be in there somewhere, it might just need a little tweaking to form the basis of a clear and simple statement.

Every single person who reads the text should walk away with the same clear idea. Your writing has to be clear, concise and interesting to enhance your personal brand. There are a few key universal features of strong writing:

- The hook
- The key message
- The proof
- The call-to-action

The hook is your opening sentence, a single line that will encourage people to read further. Hooks can be posed as a question or as a statement. They should be short, snappy, and thought-provoking in some way. Perhaps it is a big question that you are going to answer in the next few lines or a statement that defines exactly who you are.

The key message is an expansion of the hook. Your key message should be the single, defining thing that you want to share with the world. Effectively, you are laying out in simple terms the argument or point that you want to make. This outlines what exactly you are known for and what your niche is.

From there, you have to prove your message. Lay out the professional achievements and experience that you have that show your reader you can do what you are claiming.

Round it all off with a call-to-action (CTA). This is a closing statement that asks something of your reader: "find out more" or "get in touch to talk about how I can help you." CTAs are instructive and active. Psychologically, this encourages your reader to actively engage with what you have told them.

Using Simon Sinek's 2020 LinkedIn bio as an example, let's look at this concept in more depth. Simon writes:

"Simon Sinek is an unshakable optimist who believes in a bright future and our ability to build it together. Simon's WHY is to inspire people to do what inspires them so that, together, each of us can change our world for the better.

With a vision to change the way businesses think, act, and operate, Simon and his teamwork with leaders and organizations in nearly every industry to help transform company culture and create a better working world.

As a trained ethnographer, Simon has discovered remarkable patterns about how the greatest leaders and organizations think, act, and communicate. He is fascinated by the people and organizations that make the greatest, lasting impact on the world. He has devoted his life to sharing his thinking and leading a movement to inspire people to do the things that inspire them.

Simon may be best known for popularizing the concept of WHY in his first Ted Talk in 2009. It has since become one of the most watched talks of all time on TED.com, with 37+ million views.

Simon is a bestselling author and shares his ideas in the books Start With Why, Leaders Eat Last, Together Is Better, Find Your Why, and The Infinite Game.

Learn more at simonsinek.com."

The start of the bio is a perfect example of a hook: "Simon Sinek is an unshakable optimist who believes in a bright future and our ability to build it together." It's bold, concise and it makes you want to find out more.

Then, Simon develops his *why* and then gives a brief outline of his professional experience, of the value that he provides and to whom. Simon explains a little bit of his story, the steps that have brought him to where he is now. The effect is that it offers more credibility to his original statement.

He then lays out some of his most successful work – books and talks. This offers some proof, as well as encouraging readers to check out some of his work.

It's as simple as that. Follow this structure, always keep your key message at the top of your mind and your audience will gain the desired impression of you.

Another example is Tina Müller:

"*Tina Müller is an international business leader, author, and activist. She is a beauty industry expert (with over 20 years of experience in the field). Tina is currently the CEO of Douglas and a true innovator at heart. Always seeking novel, better and more efficient ways to solve problems and reach visions. At Douglas, she's successfully steering the #FORWARDBEAUTY strategy, leveraging new and disruptive digital technologies to ensure Douglas strengthens its number one position as a beauty destination for European customers.*

Tina is a passionate supporter of women in leadership and she strongly believes in the power of support. That's why she's a mentor and partner of the Initiative Women into Leadership (IWiL).

She is an author, future enthusiast, marketing guru and game-changer. When she's not at the office you'll find her in her urban garden or diving deeper into the topics of ageing and health."

Hook: "Tina Müller is an international business leader, author, and activist."

Once again, this is concise and to the point, but it is also an unexpected combination. It lays out the way that Tina would like to be perceived in simple, bold language.

The key message: "She is a beauty industry expert (with over 20 years of experience in the field). Tina is currently the CEO of Douglas and a true innovator at heart. Always seeking novel, better and more efficient ways to solve problems and reach visions."

The final sentence in particular explains more of Tina's values and priorities. This is impactful without being particularly extravagant and is a good example of a bio that is simple but still highly effective.

The proof: "At Douglas, she's successfully steering the #FORWARD-BEAUTY strategy, leveraging new and disruptive digital technologies to ensure Douglas strengthens its number one position as beauty destination for European customers."

Here, Tina has highlighted the project that she cares about the most. Again, it allows readers to delve deeper into her work if they are interested.

The call-to-action: "When she's not at the office you'll find her in her urban garden or diving deeper into the topics of aging and health."

This is a more subtle call-to-action, but it highlights the fact that Tina produces information about certain topics, encouraging readers to look further at her profile to find those resources.

Simon's bio is much more descriptive and emotive, whereas Tina's is more straightforward and direct. Both work because they follow the formula outlined above.

FIND YOUR KEY MESSAGE

Message is the fourth aspect of a successful personal brand. Your message should be about your impact in the world. How do you want to make the world better? In what ways do you make the lives of others easier or better? As I mentioned before, you need the right motivation, mindset, method and message to excel in personal branding. Your message is just as important as the other three aspects. If your message is off, or uninspiring, no one will pay attention to your personal brand. A great message communicates your impact in an interesting way.

Before we get into the specifics of platforms and content timelines (we will cover this in the next part), you are going to decide on your messaging. In other words, you are going to define your one key message and your views on the key topics in your area of expertise. This builds on your personal branding pillars but is focused more on your impact, your opinions, your values and your personal approach to relevant topics.

Your key message should be the single, defining thing that you want to share with the world. It is the mark you make, the value you add. Now you will develop a few brand messages that support this overall objective.

Choose the three topics closest to your heart that best illustrate what you care about and that feed into your overall key message. These should be authentic. Inauthenticity becomes obvious very quickly. Similarly, no one gains an audience by being vanilla. That's not to say you have to be divisive or controversial. You just have to have an opinion. Let your opinion and your knowledge inform your messaging.

Messaging can evolve over time, but I would recommend sticking with a few clear ideas, so your personal brand doesn't become confusing to others.

For example, my personal brand centres around communications and personal branding. My key message is that every organisation or person can take control of their reputation to achieve their goals. That is my impact on the world. I want to help others make the most of their potential. I also share expertise and insights based on my unique approach to personal branding. My messages include "today communication is a hard skill", "reputation precedes profit" and "becoming unignorable with a personal brand is the key to professional success". All of my professional content online is in some way affiliated to these topics and shares my clear stance on the issues.

Marie Kondo took the world by storm a few years ago with her book, *The Life-Changing Magic of Tidying Up*. She created the Konmari method – an entirely unique take on a topic that many would find dull – and her passion allowed others to be enchanted by her vision. Marie's one key message is that tidying up can be life changing. Marie's messaging focuses on ease, taking pleasure out of the small things, and making time for what matters to you. These messages enable readers to envision an easier and more fulfilling life. Marie is now an icon, simply for teaching people how to tidy their homes in a new way. That is the power of strong messaging: it allows your audience to buy into your vision.

Tom Bilyeu, CEO of Impact Theory, also has one key message: he believes that anything is possible with a growth mindset. His messaging focuses on high performance, the value of hard work and finding your passion. This message inspires and motivates his followers to work harder (and smarter) at the things that they truly care about. They are smaller, complimentary aspects of the overall message.

Your messages should allow others to understand your worldview. This will allow you to draw in an audience that shares a certain outlook. Think about the value that you would like to give to your audience and formulate messaging that will contribute to that.

Using the brand pillars that you wrote down in chapter four, write down the brand messages that best reflect your views and values. They will form the basis of your content production.

Whenever you feel like you have nothing to say, come back to these messages. They will provide the core of your content and allow you to build an audience that shares your passions and values.

WRITE YOUR PITCH

You can now write your very own personal statement following this structure: hook, key message, proof and call-to-action.

Once completed you will have a personal narrative that is compelling and that demonstrates the value that you provide for others. This means that anyone reading your LinkedIn, website, pitch deck or job application will have a clear understanding of the person behind the list of experiences.

Your personal statement also serves as the basis for your verbal pitch that you can use to introduce yourself in conversations, at events, in the elevator or whenever someone asks about you or your business. Practice your pitch, and make sure you can deliver it flawlessly each time.

TELL YOUR STORY

To complement your pitch, your personal back-story is a huge part of developing relationships with your audience. Adding personality to everything you do will also help you increase your visibility and cut through the noise online. You have your brand statement, laying out your experience and values to others. This makes you an asset, and that is a step in the right direction. But to have a brand, you need to make yourself relatable, likeable, and trustworthy. Your brand is the heart and soul of your reputation. Telling your story creates context and justification for your actions and experiences and allows other to emotionally invest in you. Your statement will attract the right connections, and our story will help to cement those relationships and build your 1,000 true fans.

Lewis Howes is a formidable storyteller. A former professional football player, he ended up sleeping on his sister's couch after a career-ending injury, broken and penniless. Picking himself up, he began reaching out to highly accomplished people, asking them to tell him the story of their success. These interviews gave him new direction, new inspiration and new hope. At 29, he launched his podcast, *The School of Greatness*. It has become a huge success thanks to the inspiration transpiring from his interviews. Lewis's story is humble. He came back from rock bottom and is now on a mission to help others overcome their challenges and find their greatness.

How can you replicate this kind of storytelling? First, you need to decide what story you want to tell. You already have your brand statement, but your story is the special sauce that adds flavour as you serve your insights to your audience. You have a very strong and clear written statement that outlines your values and your experience. Now you need to consider the aspects of your story that will make you unique and relatable to your audience. A degree of vulnerability and transparency goes a long way. You probably have overcome a change, a challenge or a crisis that left you transformed. You found a solution to your problem and now you want to share it with the world. You become the "guide" and your audience is the "hero".

Alexandra Ocasio-Cortez ("AOC"), the youngest American Congresswoman in history, shares her history with refreshing candour. Before her debut in politics, she worked as a bartender and waitress to help her mother to fight foreclosure on their home. She recounts these years as extremely tough but fulfilling. When she launched her campaign in 2018 for New York's Fifteenth District, she was still waiting tables.

Her gripping story stands out in politics for its authenticity. She experienced troubles first-hand and makes this a relatable experience for her voters. For AOC's followers, many of whom are from similar working-class backgrounds, she demonstrates that she is a hard-working, humble candidate who maintains the same values that she had prior to taking office. She overcame the struggle and so can they.

It can be very effective to share your story explicitly, depending on the personal brand that you are trying to build online. Linda Broschkowski, the founder of Germany's first agency for female DJs, Female Music Force, tells her personal story as part of the overall brand narrative. Detailing her experiences as one of the first female DJs in Berlin, she explains that her mission is to reduce the gender gap in DJing. Linda is visibly passionate about music in everything she does, as well as being vocally supportive of other women in music at all times. By sharing her personal perspective, Linda attracts other female DJs who have similar backgrounds, visions and frustrations about the industry. The result is both a team and an audience of like-minded individuals who strongly support Linda and her company.

Integrating your personality into your online presence humanises you and makes you more likeable. It allows people to decide whether you are "their kind of person", which elevates their relationship with your brand. They are much more likely to trust you if they believe that you share a certain perspective on the world.

Telling your story feeds into the heart and soul of your brand. It helps to develop that emotional connection with your audience. In essence, you are saying: I have overcome the problem you are facing right now, and I will help you overcome it as well. I can't emphasise it enough: having 1,000 true fans is infinitely more fruitful than one million disengaged ones. Sharing your story attracts these true fans by giving your brand depth and embellishing it with an emotional angle.

AN EVERGREEN STRATEGY

Over the summer of 2020, alongside writing this book, I interviewed the chief communicators of some of the world's most successful businesses for our *Speak Like A CEO* summer podcast series. From Sabia Schwarzer of Allianz to Mette Refshauge of Maersk, a trend began to emerge when discussing the topic of communicating in the digital age. The guests stated that the key to phenomenal communications is a brilliant strategic overview, underpinned by the skills to execute your strategy well. The future belongs to those who master both strategy and execution on a daily basis.

In this chapter, we discussed how to formulate your strategy by setting out your brand statement and messaging. These two elements are based on your goals, set out in the previous chapter, to ensure that your strategy is tailored to your personality and ambitions.

With an overall story and a clear key message, it should be very clear both to you and your future audience who you are, what you believe in and what you can add to their lives. You have also taken the time to consider your network and the skills that you have available in order to express yourself.

For the final section of this week, let's combine all of those elements into a one-sentence strategy. In the next chapters, we will explore tools and channels in great detail, so let's keep that general for now and focus entirely on the relationship you will build with your audience. To give you a few examples:

I will position myself as a thought-leader on the future of urban mobility to grow my ride-sharing business.

I will build a personal brand as a top web designer to build a team and stop exchanging my time for money.

I will become the go-to-person on smart cities to increase the number of keynote speeches and to get a book deal.

Your strategy should be focused enough to guide you, while offering flexibility for new ideas, tools and channels as you continue to develop your personal brand and your career. It should also include your business: how your personal brand will feed into business goals. This will ensure that you are always considering the bigger picture and prevent you from being distracted by the brand itself. Ultimately, your brand should always be benefiting your career and therefore your career should feature in the strategy itself.

Now it's your turn. Strategy is the way you plan to achieve your goals. Write down your strategy in a single sentence.

Your strategy needs differentiation. "Great products and service" won't cut it. The question you want to answer in your strategy is: What am I going to do differently from others in my line of business?

What should you do with this strategy? It has to inform all of the decisions you make. Think of the graph that I shared earlier: in order to maximise results your personal branding activity should always be strategic. In the next two weeks you will pick your tactics and begin creating content and connecting with others. Always place your strategy at the centre of your decision-making processes as you move forwards.

CHAPTER 6

Choose Your Tactics

"Demand for your business is driven by the quality of your reputation. Live and breathe your values to maintain control of your brand reputation." – Stacey Kehoe, author and entrepreneur.

Now that you have put in the hard work of figuring out *why* you are building a personal brand, and devised a strategy detailing *how*, week three explores *what* you can do to get there. There are so many digital platforms and tools out there. It is hard to pinpoint which ones are right for you.

This week, we will tackle step three of the 30-day personal branding framework: choosing the tactics. In the next few pages you will settle on your channels and set them up for optimum impact. By choosing two to three tactics and using them well, you can make sure that everyone who matters knows who you are and what you can do for them. In other words, you have taken the first step to becoming a thought-leader in your field.

As always, take as much or as little time as you need in this step. Perhaps you already have a clear idea as to which channels are suitable for you and your audience. Or maybe you are looking for more impactful ways to get your message across and need to test your tactics before you settle on a few. No matter your situation, do what works best for you.

SOCIAL MEDIA

There are a multitude of social media platforms available today. From Facebook to TikTok, various social media platforms attract specific audiences and are used in various ways. There is so much content out there today on social media, as I am sure you are well aware. But social media can be much more useful if used strategically for your personal branding activities.

I recommend selecting at least one social media channel as one of your tactics, as it is almost impossible to become unignorable without at least one strong social media profile. Make sure to ask yourself which platform will help you best carry out your overall strategy. In my professional life, I mainly use LinkedIn because the audience I want to reach is very active and accessible on the platform. Which social media platform is right for you and your personal brand?

Before you choose, ask yourself a few questions about who you are trying to reach. In chapter four you described your dream audience in detail. Based on that demographic, think about which channels they are most likely to be using. This will determine which platform is right for you as well as how and what to post on each. Who makes up your audience? Where are they? What are their interests? Who else is in that space? Think about how they communicate; what works and what doesn't work in the space.

If you are unfamiliar with your audience, ask a few friends or peers who might fall into that category. They can give you deep insights into the pain points your audience is facing.

These questions will also help you determine your content strategy. Content can be professional, personal or a mix of both personal and professional. If you are communicating with senior-level managers, a chummy tone may not be appropriate. However, a mixture of personal and professional works quite well if your audience is made up of tech start-up founders or employees.

Keep these questions and characteristics in mind as we look at some of the most popular digital platforms.

LinkedIn

LinkedIn is the number one professional social network out there today. Almost everyone is on it and most users are active. It is designed to help you create reciprocal connections with professionals in your industry or those who share the same interests. LinkedIn is much more a business to business tool, whereas most other social channels are better for B2C relationships and content.

My personal brand has benefitted unequivocally from my presence on LinkedIn. I have it open in my internet browser each day and I make sure to set aside ten to fifteen minutes per day to engage with content and add new connections. By doing so, I was able to add around 1,000 connections per month before moving on to deepen my network, rather than widening it.

There are three things that you should do to make the most out of LinkedIn. The first is to increase your reach by constantly adding relevant connections and interacting with them in a meaningful way. You don't have to know someone personally to connect with them on LinkedIn. If they work in your industry or in your location, the majority of users will be open to connecting with you. This is a quick and easy way to find a first point of contact with other professionals that you would like to build a relationship with.

The second thing that you should do on LinkedIn is create regular content based on your key messaging. Sharing your insights, ideas and thoughts on industry news allows your connections to build up a clear picture of your value. As we explored in the previous chapter, your key messages enable others to relate to you and trust you. Generating regular articles and posts on LinkedIn ensures that your name appears frequently in the feeds of your connections. The result is that people you may never have met can see the work that you do and the value that you could bring to their business.

The final feature of a successful LinkedIn strategy is to actively engage with your network. Always respond to comments on your own content and take time every day to engage with content created by others. Writing a thoughtful response to someone else's thoughts or announcements helps to deepen the online relationship. Your comments should be detailed and specific, responding to a particular part of the post. It's not just "thanks" or "great work". Taking this time demonstrates genuine care for what your network is doing. This can elevate superficial connections to truly supportive relationships.

Your strategy should always dictate the tone and style of your content on LinkedIn, as with all of your channels. Content that is most successful on LinkedIn is professionally focused and genuinely helpful to others. Most LinkedIn users are actively seeking out discussions on industry or workplace topics, whether it is sharing articles or videos alongside your personal take or creating your own advice articles. This doesn't mean that you should be overly general or bland. In fact, quite the opposite. Work plays a huge role in all of our lives, and as a result most people hold strong opinions on their professions. To get the most out of LinkedIn as a networking and branding tool, you should make your stance clear. This ensures that other professionals can see that you are someone who shares their values or understands their perspectives.

Take a look at Sabia Schwarzer's LinkedIn account. She is the Global Head of Communications and Responsibility at Allianz, the financial services and insurance giant. Sabia does a great job at telling personal stories that also give advice or share insights about corporate life. She shared her communications strategy with us on our podcast, *Speak like a CEO*. Sabia reminded me that "people are interested in people." Growing up in Pakistan, Sabia learned to appreciate the importance of storytelling. When she first came on board at Allianz, she made sure that her team could "win hearts" with storytelling.

Sabia also tells great stories on LinkedIn. In a post, Sabia told a story about how her team gave her an orange tree as a gift. She used the orange tree as a metaphor for how we find and grow our purpose at work. Something as simple as a story about a tree can communicate professional lessons to your audience. Your content does not need to be solely professional or tied to your field. You can find inspiration anywhere.

LinkedIn has the benefit of allowing a wide range of content formats to be shared. Sabia is clearly a great writer, and her content is largely text-based with images to illustrate her points. If you are more of a speaker, sharing videos can be a more effective way of telling stories or sharing advice. Graphic designers can use beautiful images. This flexibility means that you can entirely tailor your content to your skillset. Just make sure that you are posting regularly and interacting with others. This will ensure that your name is always near the top of other users' feeds.

Instagram

Since Instagram launched in 2010, the app has changed tremendously. Once a fun and easy way to share photos with friends, today its over one billion users have made it one of the most effective tools for personal branding. From Instagram influencers to interior designers, fitness experts and food bloggers, almost everyone who has a visual story to tell is on Instagram today. In recent years, even CEOs, large corporations and politicians have taken to the platform to tell more personal stories.

Instagram is highly visual, and its features change constantly. The platform has introduced a number of ways to tell your story, from the traditional photo grid, to stories, reels and IGTV. With such a variety of formats and users, it is important to identify what's right for you.

Many business people consider Instagram to be a waste of time. However, if you approach it in a strategic and professional way, it's actually a really exciting way to reach your audience.

What is most important to be successful on Instagram is to be genuine and human. Instagram is more personal; use that to your advantage to connect with your audience on a deeper level.

If you do choose to be on Instagram, the first decision to make is to decide how personal you would like to be. The platform lends itself to immediate, casual interaction and to sharing. That doesn't mean you have to share photos of your kids or your holidays. But it does mean you have an opportunity to show your interests outside of your industry.

My recommendation would be to find a few profiles of professionals that you really like and study them. Include thought-leaders from your industry and beyond. How much do they share? Perhaps it is exclusively work-related. The CEO of Walmart, Doug McMillon, shares photos of employees to celebrate their role in the company. Others share more personal thoughts and snippets of their life outside of work. There is no set rule, just decide where you would be most comfortable.

One example of an Instagram profile that I think really exemplifies the potential of Instagram is the account of SPANX founder Sara Blakely. She does not stick to one overarching aesthetic. Most of her photos were taken by her, not by a professional. She reposts inspirational quotes. She shares snapshots from her family life. Basically, she uses Instagram as most of us do.

But she also knows the power of her 420,000 followers. During the COVID-19 pandemic in 2020, Sara started the Red Backpack Fund to help female entrepreneurs. She posted frequently about the fund and featured stories of companies and individuals who have donated to the fund or have received assistance from the fund. Each post received thousands of likes or views and helped spread the word.

Despite a recent increase in text heavy captions, Instagram is a visual-first platform. We all know how hard people work to capture the best angle of their breakfast, or to take a selfie with perfect lighting. You should strive for visuals that stand out to attract attention.

Twitter and Facebook

Twitter and Facebook are also good options to build and showcase your personal brand. You can post your own content and share your positions on important topics. These platforms are great for engaging with the broader public. For example, if you want to build your network as a professional event photographer, Facebook is a great platform to reach your audience. If you want to grab the attention of journalists or politicians, who are constantly monitoring for news updates, head to Twitter.

Twitter offers an excellent opportunity to share opinions and generate attention for news, articles or other forms of content. For the past few years, it has moved largely towards being the primary platform for journalists and politicians, shifting away from being a priority platform for businesses. The focus on Twitter is more about current events and your take on them. This makes it a strong platform for the politically-minded.

Facebook remains a space for brands and advertisement but is diversifying to include new functions. The recent popularity of Facebook marketplace, events and private groups means more people are flocking to the platform specifically for those features. Private groups offer an excellent opportunity to connect with like-minded individuals and to generate engagement and conversation around your ideas. Often, the algorithm will highlight Facebook pages, so ensure that you share regular posts and are an active member in groups.

No matter which social media platform you use, you must clarify these three things before you start: your overall goal for the channel, your audience and how each platform allows you to share your message. These three things will help you determine whether or not a certain platform matches your strategy and style. Does your audience skew younger and prefer visual storytelling? Instagram is perfect for you. Are you aiming to become a thought-leader in the mobility industry? Head to LinkedIn to post longer-form articles. Ask yourself what audience will help you reach your goals. There's no point talking about career plateaus to an audience of young, university-age consumers. You want to be developing a following of industry professionals. But those same professionals are the wrong audience for an entrepreneur developing skincare for teenagers, for example.

YouTube

YouTube has gained huge influence in the past few years. With some YouTubers drawing in hundreds of thousands of euros for a single advertising deal, it's evident that the world of business has finally caught on to the trend.

There are a few different features that make YouTube a strong platform for building your personal brand. The video format allows your audience to feel much more connected because they can see and hear you. Recently, creators have started to publish longer videos – 30 minutes to over an hour – to take advantage of advertising roll in the middle of their content. This means that consumers are increasingly open to longer content. As such, you can take the time to go into detail with your ideas much more than in a LinkedIn post.

YouTube is owned by Google. This means that YouTube videos appear near the top of the majority of search results. With some smart video titling, such as the questions most commonly asked on Google on your subject, you can push your name and your brand to the top of relevant searches. It's important to create eye-catching thumbnails in order to draw clicks when your video appears. You should also make sure that the audio and video quality is high, although that is easy to achieve these days even with your smartphone camera. YouTube also enables subtitling, which can contribute to SEO: if you fill your video with key terms, you will bring it right to the top of the list when anyone searches for advice in your field.

There are a number of other social media channels that I haven't detailed here. I have chosen the most widely used platforms for professionals, but if you find yourself drawn to a different channel and can find an audience, don't rule it out. For the majority of solopreneurs and business owners, however, your personal brand will most likely be featured on one of the channels discussed in this section. In addition, social media platforms are constantly evolving, and new channels are likely to break through. What is available today is just a snapshot of what we may have in a few years. Choose your main channel and don't try to grow everywhere. Focus on one channel and do it well, instead of aiming for omnipresence.

Personal Websites

It is almost impossible to build a personal brand without social media. Some use it in lieu of a personal website. However, if you really want to boost your online visibility, I would suggest building a quality personal website. Social media as well as search engines are completely outside of our control. If you rely solely on social media or Google to be seen, one algorithm change can pull the rug from beneath your feet. This is not a distant threat – in fact, it has happened many times over the past decade. For instance, since a major algorithm change in 2018, it has become very hard for businesses to be seen by their own Facebook followers unless they pay for the privilege. The pattern repeats itself: a new platform makes it easy to build audiences to attract users. After a while, its strategy shifts from growth to monetisation. Advertisers take over from content creators.

Use social media to your advantage but remember that you are not in control. Hence the need for a personal website. A personal website is a digital business card and much, much more. You have complete ownership of your website. You can collect email addresses, get subscribers to your newsletter, even sell products. It can be a great depository for all of the work you want to display, all of the articles you have written, or all of the art you have created.

Websites are differentiators. They introduce your audience to your values and to your purpose. A website should keep the visitor top-of-mind at all times. From design to content, a personal website is fundamentally about who it serves.

Websites give you space to tell your own story in your own format. And today, you don't need a designer or programmer to make an appealing, easy-to-use website. All it takes is sitting down at your computer for a weekend and the end result will boost your personal brand in a number of ways.

There are a few different services that make this easy for you. WordPress, Squarespace and Wix are the most popular, and offer beautiful templates for a range of needs. Kajabi is great for hosting courses and digital products; Shopify empowers you to build an e-commerce business. The best websites are simple and visual, at least for the first page. You can put more text on the relevant subpages.

What to include on your website depends on your objective. Are you using your website to sell a product? To showcase your work? Or is it an authority site on a certain subject that shares detailed, well-researched information?

No matter what your objective is, there are a few main components that every website should have in order to boost your personal brand.

First, the homepage. Your homepage should clearly state who you are and what your purpose is. Think about your users and the information and insights they are after. Provide them with value, actionable tips and useful resources.

Secondly, include an "About Me" section. Use the tips we covered in week two on how to write about yourself to create compelling copy. This can be almost an exact replica of your LinkedIn bio or your personal story.

Thirdly, include a page with examples of your previous work. The format will depend on what you do. Showcase photographs gallery-style or link to publications that feature your writing. Include news reports on your product. Don't forget to give visitors a way to get in contact. They are interested in your great work, make it easy for them to get in touch!

If you want to include longer content, such as opinion pieces, create a separate blog section. It means that people don't have to wade through heaps of text to find out the basic information, but there is still a space for them to read more if they are interested.

A quick word on images on your website. They should be high-quality and reflect your brand aesthetic. Always choose quality over quantity. Your homepage does not need multiple images in order to show off your professional accomplishments and personal character.

No matter what you decide to include on your website, make sure it is clear, concise and visually appealing. Don't pack too much information into one page or section. Every piece of information you include on your website should be intentional and must uphold your overall purpose.

Newsletters

If you have created a personal website, the logical next step is to collect email addresses and start a newsletter. Newsletters are a great communication tool because you have complete control over the content and they allow you to get inside of your readers' personal space, that is, their email inboxes. They also have a better click through rate than many channels as your audience will have actively subscribed to your content.

You need to incentivise people to sign up to your newsletter. Offer a free resource in exchange for an email address, such as an e-book or an on-demand webinar. Or position your newsletter as the best place to receive regular, well-informed content on a particular topic or industry.

The key to a successful newsletter: give your best advice and content. Your free content determines how your audience will see you. Whether that is through compiling relevant industry news or sharing your own high-quality content, newsletters should keep readers engaged and, more importantly, subscribed. We will cover content in more detail in the final section of the book, but your newsletter content can be recycled from what you have produced for your other channels. Work smarter, not harder!

Neil Patel's newsletter on Search Engine Optimisation (SEO) is not only a great resource, but also a helpful example of simple, value-adding content. Every email I receive from Neil Patel, I open. He does not use complicated design techniques or sales language. He does redirect readers to his products, but only as a last resort and only when the offer will actually add value to the lives of his readers.

A recent newsletter he sent to his subscribers was simple, yet attention-grabbing:

"Are you tired of getting little to no traffic?

Today we are going to change that.

I have 3 homework assignments for you. In total it will take you less than 30 minutes, but if you do them your traffic will start going up."

Below that he listed the three assignments with links for each. It was that simple. But he made it immediately clear how those assignments could help me increase my SEO efforts.

Keep in mind that your subscribers don't want to be sold to. If you give them valuable resources and insights, they will continue to open and engage with your newsletter. From time to time, you can suggest that if they liked the free content, maybe they would also benefit from your other offers. Neil Patel does this in an open and smart way. His message is: Follow these steps to improve your SEO, and if you need any help, feel free to contact me.

STRATEGY FIRST, TACTICS SECOND

By now, you should have a clear idea on what tactics you will use to create your personal brand and to achieve the goals you have set out for yourself. Make sure to zero in on the platforms that will allow you to look and sound like your authentic self.

For most people, the ideal tactics will be apparent pretty immediately. It is largely about what feels natural to you, in terms of the way you communicate and the audience you want to communicate with. You can make it entirely personal: your online presence should just be a curated extension of who you really are. Building this strategy is simply about being more intentional in your approach.

As you continue to build your personal brand, always keep in mind that the platforms you use are not your strategy. They *uphold* your strategy. They are tactics. These tactics can and should change over time based on advances in technology or user preference. However, your overall strategy that you developed in week two remains consistent.

By focusing on two to three tactics that are deeply tied to your overall strategy, you will be able to reach your target audience where they are. You will be able to build your presence and attract their attention on platforms that they also know and love. You will post content that they are interested in and will engage with. Personally, this means that I am not just on LinkedIn. I use LinkedIn as a way to maintain my personal brand and to grow my audience, and Instagram to flesh out my brand and share my personal interests. For you, this might mean posting a short story each morning on Instagram to connect with your audience on a more personal level. The bottom-line: don't just be a sender. You want to actually engage with your audience on social media to build trust over time.

Setting up various social media accounts or building a personal website is well worth your time. The effort you put in during this stage will continue to pay off for years to come. And once you have these channels set up, the fun starts. Creating content for the various platforms you are on allows you to think creatively and strategically about the topics you care most about. This is something we explore in the next chapter.

CHAPTER 7

Execute with Impact

"We learn that the more we are true to ourselves, the more we can connect with and contribute to the world." – Brendon Burchard, author and high-performance coach.

With your newfound clarity, strategy and tactics in place, we have reached the final week of this 30-day programme: executing your personal brand. Week four, or the final stage, focuses on building a system that enables you to make the most of your time. You will learn about content calendars, testing and how to pivot regularly so that your content is specifically designed for your unique audience.

A client once asked me: "How can I make people listen to what I have to say?" "Well," I said, "you can't make them listen to you. Instead, ask yourself: What can I do to make my target audience want to follow me?" The answer is: make your contributions valuable, entertaining and thought-provoking. We become unignorable by sharing our unique voice in the service of others.

Achieving this isn't as difficult as you may think. We are all experts in something. We all have a special set of skills and a specific knowledge base that we can share with others. We all have opinions that can be of use to others. If we make an effort to understand our audience, we all have the capacity to become thought-leaders in our industry. Specifics on growing an audience are included in the next chapter.

OBJECTS IN MOTION TEND TO STAY IN MOTION

I am going to take you through one of the simplest methods for creating strong, consistent content that can fill your different channels on a weekly basis. The basic premise involves writing or recording one longer piece of content, which is then repurposed in a variety of ways for different channels.

Then, you will learn all about scheduling, and how to ensure you have an active presence on your different channels without investing an excessive amount of time. Ideally, this will mean you dedicate an hour every few weeks to generating ideas, but it will appear to others as if you are constantly present on different platforms. The result is that your name will be a strong presence online, without having to invest too much time.

I know what you're thinking, this must be an hours-long task that has to be completed each day. I won't lie to you: I invest a fair amount of time in growing and maintaining my personal brand. However, I do not play the volume-game. I don't post aimlessly and with no goal in sight. With strong systems in place, I ensure that this time is spent on activities that I find enjoyable and entertaining, while getting the maximum ROI. We already spend a lot of time streaming, reading emails and consuming social media content. Become a producer instead, and those minutes will be so much more valuable to you personally and professionally.

I am personally committed to producing content every working day, be it posting on social media, writing a book or recording a podcast or video. If you follow this simple guideline, content production quickly becomes a powerful habit that replaces content consumption. Would you rather spend 30 minutes a day building your brand and or passively scrolling through Instagram?

The bottom line: consistent, audience-centric content will ensure that your brand attracts the people that you want to work with.

On-point articles and value-adding interactions work to boost your personal brand. Soon, you won't have to push your message as hard, people will be coming to you instead. The amount of effort you have to put into sustaining your brand will not always be massive, but effort remains important. Afterall, you want to be known as the expert in your field for years, not just for a few days.

Blogger Tim Denning put it best:

"Content equals freedom.

Content helps you find what you're looking for in life. Content helps you narrow your thoughts. Content helps you clarify and see your ideas in a new light. Content helps you meet people. Content helps you create conversations. Content helps you find work you enjoy. Content helps you validate a business idea. Content helps you find customers. Content helps you change your life.

Content, content, content .... will hack your life in your favour."

There are a few tricks to get your content seen once you start creating it regularly. These rely on Search Engine Optimisation (SEO) to push your brand to the top of people's searches.

BUILDING YOUR ONLINE PRESENCE THROUGH SEO, PART 1: YOUR NAME

Is all of this digital effort really necessary? I will answer with a resolute "yes", and here's why: content creation and execution is vital to developing that sense of context that I mentioned in the introduction. It is the quickest and easiest route to developing an active online presence. Regular content positions you within the world in real time. It demonstrates an awareness of current industry changes, people and events in your local ecosystem and local or global trends. It is much easier for a client or customers to trust someone who seems educated and active within their industry.

Often, when people come across you online, it is a second touchpoint. They have probably already met you at a conference or an event, or even a social setting. Maybe you were recommended by a contact. When they are looking for you online, this continuous content production builds upon that first interaction that you had. It adds to their impression of you.

To this end, you want to ensure that you are easy to find online. The aim of a search engine is to help you find the most relevant and accurate information as quickly as possible. To rank at the top, you need to establish yourself as the most trusted source of that information, so that users are directed to your sites first.

I recently had lunch with a prospective client, to whom we were recommended. Before our meeting, he looked at my channels and discovered my books and our podcast. Based on what he found about me, he had already decided that we could help him with the coaching and positioning of his CEO.

Search Engine Optimisation makes sure that your personal brand will be seen and admired by those who matter most to you. SEO is a great place to start in order to gain an understanding of the more technical reasons why producing digital content is important. Investing in SEO will help your name show up on the first page of Google when someone searches your name. This isn't gaming the system: it's about understanding how search engines function and acting on those learnings. The recent rise in SEO-dedicated positions at many companies demonstrates how vital the skill is becoming as we become reliant on digital search engines for almost everything that we do.

Take a second and search your name. What comes up? If you have a very unique name, you might be lucky to already appear prominently on Google. Apologies to those with more common names, you will have to work a little harder.

The first stage of SEO will involve a clean-up. With so much information available online, we all have a long digital trail as a result of many, many years of online activity. It is very important to make sure that there is nothing currently available to the public that could damage your personal brand. This could be a major reputational issue, a mistake from many years ago, or simply a few social media accounts that are no longer representative of how you would like to be perceived. I do SEO audits like this for clients all the time. It's important to take stock of every part of your online existence and clean it up as necessary.

Take the time to really search through and see what comes up. Articles, videos, accounts, comments, automated messages, even reviews on Amazon. You don't want to risk losing out on a job or a client as a result of an old video or an overly defensive restaurant review. It sounds over-the-top, but there are countless cases of someone's past mistakes coming back to haunt them. Go through the search results with a fine-tooth comb and delete or shut down anything that doesn't serve your new personal brand. These audits will help you track progress but will also alert you to any negative – or positive – developments.

Now that you have cleaned out everything that you don't want people to see, you need to maximise the things that you want them to see. The goal with SEO is for your brand and your key message to fill the first page when others Google your name. That mean that you are in control of the information that others find out about you.

The first step is to make sure that your name, when searched, draws users to your profiles. Upload plenty of high-quality photos that carry your name in the file description. You can also buy the Google Adword of your name and link it back to your website. This will rank your site above any other when someone searches for your name. Active social media accounts also rank highly on Google.

Finally, getting your name featured in the media is excellent for SEO. I delve into media coverage later in this book, but it is important to know that media outlets rank at the top of many search results. If your name is cited in an article, it will not only highlight your expertise in a field, but also boost the visibility of your profile online.

BUILDING YOUR ONLINE PRESENCE THROUGH SEO, PART 2: YOUR TOPIC

With your name at the top, you have to ensure that your key message is there alongside it. You will have to optimise all of your digital content. While top search engines continuously change how they rank pages to keep marketers and others from bypassing the algorithms, there are some universal truths to stick to. It comes down to making your website, or other pages related to your name or personal brand, a trusted source of information.

What does this entail? Make sure the information on your website is always up to date. Take time each month to update content. Add high-quality pictures and make sure to add your name in the titles so that these images come up when people search for you in image search engines. This content should always focus on your key message. With articles, put your key message somewhere in the title. If you create YouTube videos, the title and thumbnail should be highly relevant to your personal brand. YouTube videos always rank high on Google searches, so this is a particularly good trick.

Across all content, make sure to use a handful of keywords that people will associate with your personal brand. By this I mean pick a few terms that sum up your content neatly and use them throughout your posting. These terms shouldn't be too niche – they need to be words or topics that someone else would search for – but also not so general that you get drowned out. For my personal brand, I aim to feature words such as "brand identity", "brand pillars", "reputation management" in my content. You want to be the result that appears first when people are looking for related services. An easy way to do this is to buy keywords in your Google Ads campaign, so that your ad will show up at the top of the results page when someone searches for that term.

Now, this can be cheap, or it can be very, very expensive. Basically, you are bidding for your keyword of choice. You will have to place a high bid to show up at the top of results for "marketing". However, if you choose something more niche, you will spend less and receive more targeted traffic. Do some research on the words your target audience uses. What questions are they asking? How are they phrasing their questions? Besides Google, you can use tools such as Ubersuggest or Answerthepublic.com to help you out.

Once you have determined the best keywords to use, include them in all of your content. I would advise against doing this in an obvious way but try to place them strategically. Do not try and incorporate the same keyword a dozen times in a single blogpost, as your content will be penalised for keyword stuffing. Think about reader experience – who wants to read five paragraphs with one word repeated in every other line? Ranking is also determined by the amount of time a user stays on your page, so make sure your content is highly engaging. A rule of thumb is to focus on one or two keywords per piece of content, and to use them wisely.

One trick that can boost the visibility of your post is to insert these keywords where the readers can't spot them, but the search engine can. This includes the URL, the meta description, the pictures or the title tag. Use your keywords with parsimony in your text body, but don't hesitate to bombard the backend descriptions.

It is your goal to become synonymous with the keywords you use. I suggest focusing on the four places where we search for professionals: Google, YouTube (videos), Amazon (books) and LinkedIn. When someone searches for your name or related keywords, your profiles and website need to be among the first results. People will quickly give up searching if your content is buried beneath a pile of superfluous results.

At this stage, I suggest you carry out a short audit of the questions people are asking about your topic. You can buy Adwords and identify the keywords to be included in your content.

EXECUTING YOUR PERSONAL BRAND

Producing online content – both for your brand image and relevance – is key. To take this to the next level, this final week will be about the specifics of that content. Tone and style are as much a part of personal branding as the topic, because they also offer insights into your personality. However, you don't want to find yourself spending hours and hours obsessing over different posts for different channels every single week.

The key to content creation is to optimise one big idea for lots of content.

Over the past few years, I have developed a system for creating valuable content online. Every few weeks, I take an hour to write down the different ideas that I have been thinking and learning about recently. Writing it down is really important: it allows you to organise your thoughts into something more coherent and more valuable for others.

I either write an article or a script which is turned into a five- to ten-minute video that can be shared on YouTube and LinkedIn. At first this might seem like a daunting task, but you will quickly realise that you easily have enough content: we are constantly thinking and developing our ideas. Just think about how many thoughts you have in a day! If even a small percentage of these are related to your key topics (and they will be), then there is already a large volume of information for you to use.

So now I want you to choose something that you have been thinking about recently that relates to your key topics.

This is how you turn that into a great piece of content for you audience.

The structure is much the same as the structure we used to help you write about yourself:

- Hook
- Key Message
- Proof
- Call-to-action

Recently, I wrote a piece about podcasting on my blog. It was a text that complemented a video that I recorded on the subject, and that I used for my weekly newsletter. Below, you can find an abbreviated version:

Hook: Why you should launch a podcast? (Or not)

Key Message: Podcasts are an intimate medium that create trust.

Proof: Podcasts are sought out by educated and affluent consumers for entertainment and education. As a host or guest, they give you quality time with an audience and an opportunity to position yourself as a trusted expert in your field.

Call-to-action: Two years ago, my colleague Lena and I launched our very own podcast. Eighty episodes later, *Speak Like A CEO* is still a passion project. If you are interested in how some of the world's best leaders and communicators build their reputation, you can listen to it on Apple or Spotify.

You are giving advice and offering your audience something of value. If you are doing it right, your audience will implement your advice in their business. You want to help others and become their trusted advisor. Don't just share your opinion, instead be valuable.

Nonetheless, opinions are still important. Taking a clear stance means that others can more actively engage with your thoughts, whether they agree or disagree. The other important effect is that it allows people to see your values and personality much more. In a digital age, people seek out clients, employees and service providers that share their ethos. Taking a clear stance will ensure that like-minded people are drawn to you and your work. These are the connections that could turn into work and opportunities. The next chapter will cover connections and audiences in more detail.

MAKE PERSONAL BRANDING A PERSONAL HABIT

What separates the professional from the amateur when it comes to sustaining a personal brand is that professionals plan ahead. Content calendars are your secret weapon here.

Content calendars help keep you on track and ensure that you sustain the personal brand you worked so hard to build.

A little effort goes a long way with content calendars. They are the go-to tool for anyone who wants to be successful on social media. Most professionals use a monthly content calendar that spans all of their channels and all of their content. For example, I would create a content calendar for the month of July that includes content for my podcast, my website, my newsletter, for LinkedIn, for Instagram and for Twitter.

Content calendars help keep us on track. You can carefully plan each piece of content your produce to ensure that you are adding value.

This was my calendar for the month of July. It summarises my pre-planned content which I complement with spontaneous ideas and contributions. While July was a light month because of the summer holiday period, you can already see how I strategically prepared for the book launch by covering some of the subjects outlined in this book.

Week	Monday	Tuesday	Wednesday	Thursday	Friday
1		Send newsletter: "15 minutes to your perfect bio". Post video on YouTube	Tweet on the bootcamp	Adapt newsletter content for the blog	Share podcast episode #69: Insa Klasing, CEO of TheNextWe. Post on Twitter & LinkedIn
2	Share Insiders Podcast from Oxford University Media Society on Instagram	Share insights from Insiders Podcast on LinkedIn	Send newsletter: "Quickest way to define your brand". Post video on YouTube	Adapt newsletter content for the blog	Share podcast episode #70: Konstanty Sliwowski, CEO Caissa. Post on Twitter & LinkedIn
3		Send newsletter: "3 strategies to grow your brand". Post video on YouTube		Adapt newsletter content for the blog	Launch Summer Podcast, Expert on Expert. Podcast episode #71: Sabia Schwarzer, Global Head of Comms at Allianz. Post on Twitter & LinkedIn
4	Instagram story: "How long does it take to build a personal brand"	Instagram post: "How long does it take to build a personal brand"	Send newsletter: "Don't do these 6 things if you're building a brand". Post video on YouTube	Adapt newsletter content for the blog	Share podcast episode #72: Sigrid Dalberg-Krajewski, Head of Corporate Comms at Delivery Hero. Post on Twitter & LinkedIn

Similarly, you can plan a theme for the week or the month, write a long-form piece for your website or LinkedIn at the beginning of the period and then repurpose that content for shorter posts on your other platforms. You can later complement this with an ongoing show or format like a podcast. Especially if you have taken the time to develop a unique format for your audience, you will already be generating a high number of useful ideas. Devise your content calendar around this main format, and then repurpose the content across your channels. It is as easy as that. One long piece can be repurposed all month long.

Always stick to your strategy when planning your content. If necessary, go back to the messaging that you wrote down in week three and every month plan a different piece of content for each of your messages. This will ensure that you are continuously feeding into each key message and developing the overall image of your brand to your audience.

Always spend at least the same amount of time promoting your content as you do creating it. You've spent the time thinking up value-adding content. Make sure others see it! Quotes from longer articles can be turned into tweets to redirect your audience back to the longer piece, for example. Simple posts linking to your other content can be easily added into your content calendar wherever you see a glaring gap. Don't be afraid to repurpose your ideas for multiple channels, as long as you give your best advice. If you find yourself falling behind, enlist the help of an accountability buddy to help you stay on track.

Over time, you will start to develop some really great content based on getting to know your audience and their needs. But if you are stuck for ideas at the start, I have a few suggestions for jumping off points. There are a few templates that professionals in every professional field out there use to produce engaging, interesting content month after month:

- **Top questions:** Think about the questions you asked yourself about a certain topic when you first became interested in it or that you get asked by others. Here are some examples: What is value-based recruiting? When will autonomous vehicles actually be used by the public at large? How will voice technology change the face of e-commerce? Check Google and use the most commonly asked questions as headlines. This also does wonders for your SEO.

- **Secrets for your industry:** You are an expert in your industry. Share your top insights into how the sausage is made.
- **Events:** Did you recently go to an industry event? Make the most out of your visit by telling your audience the latest trends or insights. Never just post about attending events, this does not provide any value.
- **Ask your audience:** Ask some friends or colleagues what questions they have for you and then turn those into some content! Invite your audience to an ongoing conversation on the topic of choice. For example, I asked my connections to provide feedback on a few versions of the cover for this very book. I wanted to involve them in the process and they very much enjoyed it.

With your content calendar in place, it is time to schedule your content in. It is the difference between having to invest time every single day and only having to invest time every week or month. This can be a key energy saver in the personal branding process.

Scheduling can mean different things to different people. This could mean blocking off time in your calendar to make sure you sit at your desk to actually write. For many, this means using a scheduling software such as Hootsuite or Buffer. These tools will post your scheduled content for you, so you don't have to post content yourself across multiple platforms each day.

You could make the last Friday of the month your "content day" for the following 30 days. Write your long piece or pieces, come up with some tweets and Instagram stories based on that content, schedule the posts using the software of choice and sit back and relax all month long as your engaging content is posted to all of your channels.

Remember, however, to react quickly should something unexpected occur. When posts are scheduled and a dramatic world event takes place, it will look out of touch if something irrelevant pops up on your feed. In that case, I recommend pausing your scheduled posts to think about how you can express empathy and solidarity for what has just happened in the world.

By using a content calendar and scheduling tool, you will be able to stay on message and maintain a clear brand persona across all of your channels. Each piece of content should be tailored to your channel. Start with your number one channel, then repurpose the content for other, secondary platforms, if you believe it would work there as well.

Always keep your audience in mind with every piece of content you produce. Everything you publish across all of your channels has to provide value. Your goal is to grow your personal brand, not to confuse your audience with off-topic articles or content that is not useful. If you maintain a steady stream of high-value content, your audience will grow. You will see results.

You might be thinking, "why should I focus so much on producing content when there is already so much out there?" Firstly, we are not playing the volume-game, trying to get as much content out as possible. It simply won't get seen. We are being strategic about each and every piece of content. Secondly, most digital content produced these days is of low quality and is not meant to last. Clickbait articles mostly exist to sell advertising or random products. You will be better than the boring average in your industry. Your value-adding content will stand out, attract clients or customers and help you build a lasting personal brand.

All of this work will also get your brand seen by the people who actually matter to you and your business. Putting out the right message and adding value to the lives of your audience members will put you on the radar of the employers or companies that you want to work with.

TEST AND PIVOT

Different audiences respond well to different formats and styles, so it is always worth testing, tracking and reassessing what people find interesting and helpful. I keep a spreadsheet, where I insert the headline, topic and image of the posts, and keep track of the engagements that each one has received. You can do this informally, by keeping an eye on the content that people respond well to but having the data in front of you can be helpful.

Every week or month, I would recommend testing a different aspect. For example, one month you might test different headline formulas, to see which generate the most attention. The next, you might test the colours that you use or different types of images (such as graphics, photographs and simple text). In a different month, you could test length of posts. There are some great headline testing tools such as CoSchedule and Sharethrough, that analyse your headlines for you based on algorithms that test clickability. Websites such as Optimizely also offer options for A/B testing content, where two variants of your content are shown to users and statistical analysis is used to determine which variation performs better amongst your audience. These tools can cut out a lot of the work of collecting and analysing your own data.

While testing one aspect, keep the others largely the same. Over time, you will build a deep understanding of what content works best for your audience, and this ensures that you can continually produce content that your audience finds valuable. This is an ongoing process. Trends change. Your audience will change.

Over time, creating, testing and pivoting becomes a habit and you will see that the results are worth the extra effort.

EXECUTING YOUR PERSONAL BRAND IN REAL LIFE

A successful brand exists online and offline. It combines the best of both, allowing many touchpoints with your network. Those that you meet in person at events might look you up online afterwards and vice versa. Those that find you online can head to events that you plan on attending, speaking at or hosting to find out more and meet you in person. Use what you have built online to make valuable connections in your daily life. The best places to make these connections are at industry events such as conferences or trade shows. People who engage with your content will most likely be in attendance.

Make a commitment to go to a certain number of relevant events per month. Before I go to any event, I browse my social channels to see if any of my connections are attending. I will ask them to meet up in person at the event, or casually approach them on site. This is your chance not only to show them that your personal brand is a true reflection of who you really are. It is also a chance to see if they are as equally authentic. Crucially, this should never be done in the transactional way of traditional networking. It's about connecting. I always try to provide an interesting piece of information or insight without expecting anything in return.

I recommend you research on the speakers and exhibitors. Maybe you are not connected to these valuable contacts online, but events are a great way to make a real connection. Approach them at the event. You already have something to talk about! A brief conversation will lead to an exchange of contact details. Make sure to follow-up shortly after the event. Do this the same day or the next morning so that you are top of mind. Don't simply let your business card gather dust on their desk.

You can also become a facilitator of a group. For example, I facilitate a monthly meetup for my university alumni group in my city. This is a great way to meet people who have something in common while making valuable professional connections. This only requires a small monthly commitment, mainly maintaining an email list and reserving a table at a local restaurant or pub.

Another great idea is to organise your own event or meetup. Think up a good reason to bring together people you are interested in. This could be a panel discussion with experts or even after-work drinks. Make sure you gather contact information and thank everyone who came. And stay in contact! Those who came to your event are clearly interested in you and what you or your company has to say. It isn't hard to create an event on Eventbrite or a similar platform.

Bear Radio is a Berlin-based podcast production company and network. The founder and CEO Jill Beytin has built her personal brand around the power of podcasting to share your ideas and values. She frequently hosts podcasting events and meetups for her community. These can be simple networking events, panel discussion or training sessions for different aspects of podcasting. As a result, she has built a broad network of fellow podcasters and podcast enthusiasts. More than that, by offering helpful and informative workshops, she has made herself the go-to person to ask about anything related to podcasting in Berlin. By helping to connect others, she has managed to also find an audience for her own brand.

As always, make sure the connections you make are about adding value. Do not approach people with the intention of selling. They will not listen to what you have to say and will see you from then on as a salesperson, not a valued connection.

BUILD YOUR SYSTEM

Executing your personal brand requires a big-picture perspective. From your tactics to your online and offline interactions, there is a lot to consider in order to really curate a strong and wide-reaching personal brand. To minimise the amount of thought this takes and maximise results, you have to create a system.

Part of it is to decide when and how you will create content. Whether it's mornings, evenings, Sunday afternoon, you should pick a time that you can be creative without distraction. Block it out in your diary, to ensure that you really commit to content creation on a weekly basis. You also need to block out time every day for sharing smaller posts and engaging with others online. I would recommend half an hour of focused engagement every single day to see a real development in your online connections.

You should also take into consideration your offline appearances. Perhaps select one relevant meeting or event every two weeks, or weekly if you find them fulfilling. Register to the event and add it to your calendar. At first you may want to try many different events and whittle them down to the ones that really add value.

Over time, you will develop a system that works for you to execute your brand online and offline. With a small amount of effort each week or month, you can generate a large amount of content and make valuable connections.

Through all of this, remember that this can be a really fun process. This is an opportunity for you to speak and write about the things that you find interesting, the thoughts that you have been having, the value that you can bring to others. Focus on the things that you're good at and enjoy, but package them in a way that your audience finds most useful and entertaining. That is the secret to great content production.

MOVING FORWARD

Congratulations! You have successfully laid the foundations of your personal brand. Throughout this process, you have defined the *why, how* and *what* of your personal brand and developed a personal system that will allow you to execute with impact. You have defined a strategy that focuses on the value that you bring to people around you. You have formulated your messaging and chosen the tactics that you will use to share it. In a relatively short period of time, you have ensured that anyone who finds you online knows who you are, what you care about and how you can help them. This puts you in an incredibly strong position to attract the people and opportunities that you desire and deserve.

So, what now? It is important that you keep this momentum going. In the final section of this book, I show you how to take your personal brand to new heights. The skills that you have learned throughout this journey will serve you forever. As we move forwards, it is about levelling up.

PART III

BECOMING UNIGNORABLE

At this point in your journey, you have already laid the foundations to reach the goals that you laid out at the very beginning of this book. The longer you maintain this brand, the more people you will meet, opportunities you will access and benefits you will reap. In this final part of the book, I show you how to build on those foundations that enable you to take your personal brand to the next level.

This step is a bonus. What I share in this chapter is not necessary to building or maintaining a personal brand. However, these efforts will help you take your personal brand to the next level. I have personal experience with each tactic I share with you, and I know just how impactful each one is. You have the insights necessary to become truly unignorable.

Imagine your personal brand as a flywheel. After the initial effort taken to get it in motion, it continues to turn with minimal input from you.

As you hone your skills and make personal branding a habit, you can integrate both bigger and more long-term projects into your brand: public speaking, podcasting, even writing your own book. By utilising the brand that you have developed in 30 days (give or take), you can embark on some of the projects that you might have always dreamed of. With your new network and audience, you can create and share your insights in much more interesting ways that will help a larger number of people. You will raise your status from visible to remarkable, and then from remarkable to unignorable.

CHAPTER 8

Create your Ecosystem

"You can expect to be rewarded when you've built a high-performing ecosystem that delivers value." –Daniel Priestley, author of Oversubscribed.

The next step is to use your personal brand to create opportunities that demonstrate your expert-level knowledge in your field. This chapter will give you the key strategies for continuing to develop and curate your personal brand in a way that brings your unique perspective to a committed audience. In doing so, you will learn how to reinforce your status as a trusted advisor, thus making you indispensable to your clients in any eventuality. You will elevate yourself from remarkable to unignorable.

In his book, *So Good They Can't Ignore You,* Cal Newport writes about "The Law of Remarkability". He describes it as follows: "For a mission-driven project to succeed, it should be *remarkable* in two different ways. First, it must compel people who encounter it to remark about it to others. Second, it must be launched in a venue that supports such remarking." You may have a remarkable idea about your industry, but it won't gain traction unless you share it within your industry via the right channels, be it a major conference or specific Facebook groups.

With your personal brand in place, you can now dedicate your time to creating something remarkable for your dream clients or your target audience. Your goal is to create an ecosystem surrounding your personal brand.

What exactly is a business ecosystem? An ecosystem includes everything and everyone who touches your personal brand or business. This includes your existing clients or customers, all of your content or sales channels and any awareness-raising activities (I will explain how to raise awareness more in chapter ten). It also includes each and every touchpoint that people have to get in contact with you, be it your search results, social media channels or your personal website. In my case, this extends to my books, the *Speak Like A CEO* podcast and my blog.

The overall goal is directing people to your products and services and offering them exceptionally high-value work. All of the other touchpoints feed into this overall aim. Your online channels and offline opportunities allow you to deepen the relationship with your ecosystem, building trust that can be converted into business.

A business ecosystem will allow you to share your insights and solve your customers' problems under the umbrella of your personal brand. You can offer multiple products or solutions related to your brand that will work to boost your reputation and develop this trust. By now, you have internalised how to attract an audience with your unique perspective and continue to create content designed to be genuinely useful for your new connections. By constantly offering value to your current network as well as sharing a vision that they can relate to, they will be much more inclined to buy future products and services.

These products and services – books, coaching, workshops, training courses or anything that fits the PAIDS model outlined in chapter two – give your customers the opportunity to engage with your business.

Donald Miller was relatively unknown before publishing his book *Building a StoryBrand.* The success of the book drew a huge amount of attention to Donald, which he converted into a following with a strong personal brand online. As he built an audience, his company grew from a marketing consultancy to a whole ecosystem, including books, podcasts and a "university" that teaches people how to market. Across each aspect of the ecosystem, he offers high-quality, relevant content that appeals to his original audience.

This is a key feature of becoming a trusted advisor. Your audience becomes engaged with everything that you produce because they value your insights holistically, rather than seeking you out for answers to specific questions. By offering a wide range of high-quality content that is in line with your overall vision and messaging, your audience comes to trust your vision and thought process as much as they trust your practical advice. This is the point at which you can convert an audience member into a long-term client.

A business ecosystem draws together many different elements of your personal brand in such a way that people buy into you holistically. With every product and service linked under the umbrella of your brand – your vision, your messaging – your audience can be sure that they will be purchasing something relevant to them. And each of these purchases will be feeding into the overall impression that they can trust you.

Gaining the trust of your customers and becoming a trusted advisor is a coveted goal in business. What is required? According to Anthony Iannarino, author of *Eat Their Lunch*, becoming a trusted advisor means you go above and beyond for your customers and clients. He writes: "If all you do is provide a good product, you will find it extremely difficult to generate any real loyalty from your clients." A personal brand and a solid business ecosystem will help you become a trusted advisor by offering your current and potential customers multiple ways to experience your expertise and your personality. People will be interested in you, value your expertise and want to buy more from you. It's a virtuous circle from which you will continuously benefit.

BUILDING YOUR COMMUNITY

If you truly want to be successful in today's digital environment, selling products and services is no longer enough. This book has demonstrated the importance of building a personal brand to fulfil your goals and to help others. To take it to the next level, I recommend thinking of building a community around you. Networks of like-minded people are an invaluable resource in any aspect of your life. If you are interested in the same idea or working towards the same goal, that community can be both supportive and motivational. Whether you are stuck on a specific issue or generally losing momentum, it can be a real game-changer to turn to others who have experienced the same problem as you. Building a community takes conscious effort but the return on investment is very high. As you provide them with valuable insights and interesting content, they become active and engaged members of your community. In return, they will trust your products and services and have the potential to become loyal clients and customers.

Marie Forleo began her professional career working at the New York Stock Exchange but left to work for several lifestyle magazines. In 2001, she began a newsletter and developed a niche around life coaching and personal development for entrepreneurs. Without ever appearing to hard sell, she uses a range of formats to share advice with her audience, through trainings, a TV show and a blog. She has built an engaged community, and has garnered an incredible amount of endorsements, with the likes of Oprah, Richard Branson and Tony Robbins. Her brand speaks to the small and the big and gives her audience the courage and confidence to create businesses from scratch.

More recently, she has started selling products and services, such as a book and an online business school for entrepreneurs. Her audience of more than 55,000 followed her and many joined her course.

To build your community, start with one person. Take a look at your pre-existing network for others who are striving for the same thing. Opening up that conversation with someone you already know can offer an interesting new perspective: they will have a decent knowledge of your backstory, and you theirs. As a result, you can offer one another personalised support. As your community grows, you can create touchpoints such as meet-ups or LinkedIn groups.

Seeing others working through the same process as you can spark new ideas and motivate you to take risks. I have built a community of like-minded professionals committed to taking their personal brands to the next level. The support and insights offered by members across a wide range of industries and professions is deeply inspiring.

GROWING YOUR AUDIENCE

Building an audience from scratch might feel like a daunting concept, but there are many people out there who want to hear what you have to say. There will be countless individuals in a similar position to you, a similar profession or industry, who are looking to find and build great connections online and in-person. These individuals will begin to stumble across your channels themselves as a result of the work that you have put it so far. However, there are many steps that you can take to speed up the process and make sure that those connections turn into your 1,000 true fans.

The basics are rather obvious: add people in your industry, engage with their content, tag your collaborators and share your posts across multiple channels that connect with one another. Join groups, participate in conversations, be an active member of your chosen platforms and throw yourself into the community, and you will start to attract others. The aim in building a valuable audience for your personal brand is to focus on quality, not quantity.

When developing new products and services you can work backwards from your ideal audience to developing your unique selling point (USP). In the first week of the 30-day programme, you took the time to visualise your target demographic. Isolating the areas of your target audience's professional lives that cause them most frustration enables you to conceive solutions for them. With your skillset and experience, what could you do that would solve their issues? How can you package your expertise in the most interesting, digestible way, to take the thought and the stress out of your audience's life? Whether it's a course, a book, a video series, a social media campaign, something will come to you.

If your audience feels that you are solving their problems, taking their needs into consideration, they will spread the word to others in a similar situation. Your audience will grow itself and trust you more deeply. They will become much more inclined to invest in future products and services, even bringing you business, because you have already proven to have their interests at heart.

ENGAGEMENT IS KEY

What makes a pop concert special? When the singer takes time to chat with the audience, to take a few selfies, even to stage dive into the crowd. Those concerts are memorable. They help create a connection between the audience and the performer. The same principle holds for your personal branding efforts.

By engaging with your connections, you let them know that you are human and that you care about their input and enjoyment. Afterall, people are interested in people. You have to engage with your audience if you expect your message to be seen and to resonate.

It does not take long to add a thoughtful comment on a post on LinkedIn or to retweet a thought-provoking article with your own take on the matter. Each interaction I have, I make sure to be genuine. Genuine engagement fosters genuine connections.

The rules of offline connections apply just the same in the online realm. Be polite, introduce yourself and ask questions about others. Be careful with sales messages or the like over these platforms. That will undercut the powerful personal brand that you are trying so hard to craft. These messages come off as automated and pushy, not characteristics you want to embody online. If you're funny, be funny. But most of all, don't overthink it. Be who you are in real life, and the right people will resonate with you.

When interacting online, it can be helpful to set some rules for yourself. I made the choice many years ago to focus on being entirely positive online. I don't make negative comments or share negative articles. This wouldn't work for everyone – journalists often have to be critical in their approach – but for a positive, optimistic person like myself, it is the only authentic approach. Think of the online community that you would like to create and behave as if that community were interacting with you in real life.

Small wins lead to big wins. This happens in two ways: first of all, those connections will recommend you to others who are seeking your services or insights. Secondly, others will see your connections interacting with you online, and – if they like your content – begin to interact themselves.

GENERATING WORD-OF-MOUTH

A recent Nielsen study has found that 74% of consumers identify word-of-mouth as a key influencer in their purchasing decisions.

Word-of-mouth is the most important factor when it comes to building a reputation you love. You can buy all the online ads your budget allows, you can optimise every piece of content for SEO, you can even become a LinkedIn Top Voice. But all of those efforts will only get you and your business so far if clients and contacts do not talk about you or your business. You want them to recommend your products or services to their friends.

Surprise your clients or customers by over-delivering. Promise them 80% and deliver 100%. Your delighted customers will be sure to tell their friends and colleagues about the wonderful experience they had with you and your brand. A job well done is not enough. People don't talk about your hard work unless they are positively delighted.

I recently gave a presentation workshop to a large, up-and-coming company. Everyone involved was really happy with the outcome. But I wanted to delight them, not just leave them happy. The next day, I called up the head of the company and offered a free refresher session for the team after a month. I also offered to help with their presentation slides.

They didn't expect the extra help. Had I included that in the original package, they would not have been surprised. Instead, the team was positively delighted, and I forged a long-lasting collaborative partnership. Delighted customers and clients will return, building you a base of highly sought return customers. Note how easy this was: a well-timed goodie turned a one-off project into a long-term relationship. Sure, it cost me a few extra hours: a small investment compared to the effort it takes to win a new large client in my line of business.

If you want to go one step further, you can set up a referral programme, where you incentivise clients to recommend you to their peers.

Brands either grow or wither, depending on how willing we are to invest in them continuously over an extended period of time. Word-of-mouth turns your personal brand into a growth engine for yourself and your business. Set your sights on becoming a trusted advisor by developing a unique business ecosystem that generates interest and income. Through a mixture of content creation, audience engagement and deepening relationships with your dream clients, you can convert a connection into a client or customer. And if you truly delight them, they will keep on coming back for more, as well as telling everyone around them that could benefit from your work or content. Constantly strive to help your network, and they will turn to you over anyone else when you can meet their needs.

CHAPTER 9

Own Your Platform

"Everything is figureoutable." – Marie Forleo, author and entrepreneur.

In the previous chapter, I made the case for building a community of like-minded people who engage with your content but with who you also take the time to exchange with. Your audience values your insights, but they also value your genuine commitment to them. This chapter explores some of the more advanced tools available to you, that you can use to share your insights and become unignorable to your network of true fans.

As with all aspects of personal branding, your approach to levelling up should be personalised and focus on the channels that energise you, rather than drain you. The right channels will feel obvious, because you know what you like. Don't be turned off by a lack of experience or skills. Draw on the mindset approach that we discussed in Part I: turn your concerns into motivation to learn new skills or find others who can fill the gap.

YOUR UNIQUE PLATFORM

A social media following is no longer enough to set you apart from the other users on each platform. It won't make you unignorable. In order to reach the level of a trusted advisor or thought-leader, it helps to do something special. This is where the Marie Forleo model that I described in the previous chapter comes into play. Developing a format or series of formats that becomes emblematic of your brand as a whole allow you to reach the point of being unignorable.

A unique platform that entirely encompasses your strategy and messaging is an asset. Have your own show, if it enhances your brand. For me, this was *Speak Like a CEO*, the podcast and later book. I wanted to help people share their unique voice with the world, and so I centred my brand around a podcast that explored how successful leaders communicate. Our podcast is unique and targets CEOs, founders and communications professionals. Both our guests and the listeners are extremely relevant for our business.

For Marie Forleo, this was her TV show, with episodes giving specific advice on what it is to become a successful entrepreneur. Developing a unique format is key to become unignorable and to take your brand to the next level.

The most important consideration, regardless of channel, is the platform itself: your USP. Building an audience of true fans requires you to offer something personal and authentic. To become unignorable, either present yourself in a unique way and offer something that others are not doing, or improve on what is already out there. "Most recognised experts achieved success not because of some special genius, but because they learned how to put disparate elements together and present ideas in a new and meaningful way", writes Dorie Clark in *Reinventing You.*

There is no one-size-fits-all recommendation here, but I recommend an approach to generating ideas that will ensure your platform meets success. Once again, this is about your audience and not yourself.

PODCASTS

Podcasts are an incredible medium for the digital age. Strong content can come in many different forms, but many consumers now seek out long-form media. We have spent a decade with short tweets or YouTube videos, gradually reducing our attention spans. Now, research shows that a large proportion of educated and affluent consumers are actively seeking out highly produced, long-form podcasts to entertain and educate them. This is a very strong market to tap into. Thinking long-term, if you can inspire this demographic and encourage them to share your vision, you will be able to build mutually beneficial relationships with rising stars in your industry. When someone truly emotionally engages with a brand, you have their ongoing attention. Think of podcasts like Rob Moore's *The Disruptive Entrepreneur* or Lewis Howes' *School of Greatness*: they become a part of their audiences' identity, and they continue to support and share their ethos for a very long time. They form a community.

Podcasting offers more intimacy and immediacy than, for example, long articles. By lifting the words off the page and into the ears, storytelling or information sharing is given a new dimension. People listen to podcasts while cooking, exercising or commuting, which gives you more time with your audience than any other form of content. It is estimated that the spoken word is two to three times more effective than the written word. If you want to position yourself as a trusted advisor, podcasts are an excellent place to demonstrate your expertise.

There are two ways to use podcasting for your personal brand. The first is to be a guest on a podcast. The advantages are that you can reach an entirely new audience and take advantage of the listener base that someone else has built.

The most effective podcast episodes are inspirational and conversational. In a highly curated online world, listeners respond well to people who seem genuine and interesting, but not overly polished. A good podcast host will ask questions that let the guest shine. And a great podcast guest will speak with enthusiasm on the things they care about and help others, sharing opinions and insights that others may not have.

If a listener likes you, they will have a look for other things that you have done and come across your personal website or social media profiles. And at the end of the talk, the host will ask you if you have anything exciting lined up, which gives you a chance to mention your latest products, ideas or website.

The second way to use podcasting to your advantage is to create your own, and this is what I did. With my colleague Lena, I have spent two years interviewing founders and CEOs for our podcast *Speak Like a CEO.* We talk about communications and leadership, and often delve into topics such as company culture and innovation.

Hosting your own podcast has many advantages. The most important is that it allows you to have insightful conversations with people in your industry and build relationships with them. You can learn from others, develop new ideas and implement them into the way you work. In more concrete terms, it also gives you an excuse to meet and get to know new, exciting people, almost like the ultimate networking tool. While potential guests might not go out of their way to meet a total stranger for a coffee, being invited to appear on a podcast guarantees them a return on their time. This greatly increases the chance that they will be willing to meet.

And not only can you meet them, you have half an hour to have a meaningful discussion and talk about what you're good at. Obviously, it's important not to take the spotlight away from your guests, but a two-way conversation about your field of expertise helps to cement your reputation, both with your guest and your audience. If you have a podcast on the subject, your expertise in the field appears much more legitimate, as you have the content to prove it.

Examples of great podcasts abound, but I urge you to listen to a few episodes of *The Elevate Podcast*, hosted by entrepreneur Robert Glazer. He invites top-tier leaders, CEOs, entrepreneurs and thinkers to talk about how they made positive changes in their lives and businesses.

It is clear that Robert does his research about his guests before he talks to them. He brings up stories or information on whoever he is talking to. If you choose to host a podcast, be prepared to spend time doing the same. Do research on your guest, check out their social media channels and read the most recent news stories on them. Coming to a conversation armed with personal information will allow you to produce a more thoughtful, interesting and informative episode.

Developing a podcast isn't for everyone, but also not as tough as you think. There are a few very key areas that you should get right, and after that it's a lot of fun. It does take time and energy to develop the ideas, record the episodes and market them, but for me and many other podcasters this is an enjoyable and rewarding experience. And the ROI is very high: growing your network, gaining your listeners' trust and proving your expertise are the keys to enhancing your brand, after all.

First of all, nail down the topic and the format: what do you want to talk about and how do you want to talk about it? What makes it special so that it will attract an audience? An interview is the easiest in terms of production. But if you are more creative, why not try a storytelling style? Whatever you choose should feel exciting for you, because that excitement will be felt by your audience.

After that, the keys to a strong podcast are the three P's: people, production, promotion.

Great guests make life a lot easier. And the good news is that people love to be invited on podcasts, so you can actually aim quite high with your invitations. When reaching out, explain the concept and ask if they would be interested in appearing. If they're a good fit, the chances are that they'll say yes. Think about who you would actually like to speak to, and learn more from, and just ask them.

High-quality audio recordings are vital, and it's easy to achieve for a fairly low cost these days. We use the Yeti Blue mics that are favoured by many podcasters. They pick up a lot of background noise, so make sure you record in a quiet place, but the sound quality is excellent.

Choppy editing is very off-putting. If you know how to edit audio, try to make the cuts as smooth as possible. There are a lot of highly informative, free videos available on YouTube teaching the fundamentals of editing. If you don't have the time to learn, you can hire a freelance audio editor to ensure a very high-quality end-product. There are some podcasts that publicise the conversations completely uncut, but you have to be a good conversationalist to pull this off.

Finally, promoting your podcast is much the same as promoting anything else. To ensure the visibility of your podcast, as much effort should go into the promotion as into its production. Use Canva, the free design tool, to create a visually appealing graphic, or pay someone to do it for you. Pick a clear, snappy title, and a strong, energetic theme song. You can either publicise the podcast on your own social media channels or create separate ones for the podcast. I would do the former if you are just starting out, and wait until you have a large listenership to launch dedicated social media channels for your podcast. This provides a positive feedback loop, so you can build an audience in both directions.

We use Anchor for distribution, which is free and very easy to use. You simply upload the audio, title and a description, and it puts your podcast everywhere.

BECOME AN AUTHOR(ITY)

Closely tied to podcasting, books are an excellent way to demonstrate your expertise and become an authority in your field. They are a true differentiator.

My first book, *How to Speak Like a CEO*, was written as a result of the first series of our podcast. In the podcast, we interviewed CEOs and founders from a broad range of companies on communications and leadership. I developed those conversations into a series of chapters, each focusing on a different area of communications. The result was an example-based guide to communications, inspired by successful leaders across the globe.

Books are a huge part of my personal brand. I love to read, so it felt like a natural next step for me to start writing my own, based on the insights that I had gathered over the years. Writing a book allows you to sharpen your thinking on a particular topic, which makes you a much better advisor for your team and your clients. It gives you credibility, which is a very important feature of being perceived as a trusted advisor.

A book is also a business card on steroids. When I meet potential clients, I give them a copy of my second book, *Mastering Communications*. This allows them to understand my process when it comes to communications, so that they have an insight into the way that I work and approach my role. Within a few chapters, they will have a strong sense of whether or not I am the right fit for their company, which can be incredibly helpful for reaching the next step of a professional partnership.

The way that I approach writing is that when I have an idea, I ask myself why I would write that particular book. In my case, the aim is to build my brand and to help win clients for my business. It is not to make money from book sales. Next, I define the audience and ask myself why this audience should care about the book. I also question whether I feel passionate enough about the subject. This ensures that I stay motivated and that the writing process feels like an exploration of a topic I care about rather than another thing on my to-do-list. I proceed only if I have satisfactory answers to all these questions.

In case I decide to go ahead, I develop a plan for each chapter together with my team. What to include, what the key message should be, and why this is valuable for others. I then look at the content that I already have on the topic and see where the gaps are. It is possible to speed up the drafting process by recording each chapter and then use a transcription software to turn the audio into text.

By taking some time every week to repurpose that content and develop the thoughts into a longer form, you would be amazed at how quickly a valuable and insightful book can come together. This is a more elaborate process than creating a weekly article, but again it offers an extremely high ROI. On top of that, it can make you a greater asset to the people around you, because you have spent time truly becoming an expert on your topic in the process of writing.

Writing a book takes stamina but can be broken down into small, simple steps. If you have already been producing a lot of content – podcasts or articles – much of the thinking has probably already been done.

Owning your own platform is key to becoming unignorable. Owning your platform – be that on social media, a podcast or a self-published book – allows you to tell your own story your way. You can draft your narrative, and you can tell your audience exactly what they need to hear. Owned platforms give you the chance to be even more authentic and human. These platforms tend to encourage long-form communication, so you really do have the space and the agency to delve into a topic that is near and dear to you.

Co-hosting my own podcast and writing my own books has honestly given me great satisfaction. As a founder and CEO of a company, I still had the time to accomplish both. In fact, building my platform did not take away time and energy from my business but boosted it due to the exposure these formats bring. And I am convinced that they made me a better and more accomplished professional. Writing compels you to crystallise your thoughts in memorable ways, and interviewing CEOs on the podcast gives you access to the insights of the smartest minds.

CHAPTER 10

Raise Awareness

"Every action you take is a vote for the type of person you wish to become. No single instance will transform your beliefs, but as the votes build up, so does the evidence of your new identity." – James Clear, author of Atomic Habits.

Raising awareness of your personal brand and your business is tough work. But getting the word out is a vital step in taking your professional success to the next level and making a positive impact in the world. Owning your own channels is important, but so is tapping into larger communications networks.

What does this mean specifically? Newspapers, trade publications and event organisers have access to vast audiences that are relevant to you and already interested in what you have to offer. You can drastically increase the number of people you reach by giving an interview or speaking at a conference.

Opening yourself up to the broader public – not just your audience of peers and loyal clients – may seem intimidating. Why open yourself up to criticism or uncertainty? Not all journalists want to write a takedown piece, and not all conference attendees are hellbent on asking you tough questions. While this is always a possibility, you will reap many rewards from raising awareness strategically.

MEDIA COVERAGE

Generating media coverage has been the cornerstone of my career. As Head of Communications at easyJet, I gave over 1,000 media interviews and was constantly coming up with stories that the press would want to publish. A story in a respected media outlet can be a huge boost for your professional brand. Media coverage introduces you to a new audience and can cement your credibility in your field. Traditional media continue to be read and absorbed by millions of influential and engaged individuals every day, so a positive article has the capacity to create connections and opportunities that you couldn't find elsewhere.

The most effective media outreach is targeted to publications in your field because their audience will already be interested in your key topic. These trade publications are read by the decision-makers in your industry. You will get the attention of those who really matter.

You will not automatically gain coverage in these publications. You will have to develop a relationship with the journalists beforehand to gain their trust. They will need to see you as a source of quality information or interesting insights. Your personal brand will help you position yourself when journalists search your name after you reach out to them. They should have a strong sense of your expertise, and you can build on this in your later interactions.

If you can present an angle that is unique and refreshing, and relevant to an audience's interests, readers will search out your own content in order to learn more about your perspective and knowledge.

The best thing about media coverage is that it gives you perfect material for your social feeds and tends to generate further coverage. Amplified by social media, one well-received story leads to many more, as other outlets take advantage of the conversation around the initial article.

Generate just one article, podcast appearance or interview, and you can use that to approach other outlets.

To create media interest, you need a story that is made for the media. The development of online media shared on social channels has intensified the need for an excellent headline to attract clicks. If you develop a story that can be boiled down to a single, intriguing sentence, you're onto a winner.

Insa Klasing is the author of *Der 2-Stunden-Chef* (which translates to mean *The 2-Hour-CEO*), a business book that explores the concept of autonomy in the workplace. She was injured in a horse-riding accident while working as the General Manager of KFC Germany. Her injuries meant that she could only work for two hours a day before reaching exhaustion. Initially, Insa was concerned, but quickly began to see changes in the way that her team functioned. With increased autonomy, the team could focus its energy on the work that genuinely excited them and could make more decisions alone. This sped up the decision-making process and led to incredible business results that year.

In Germany, workplace culture has traditionally revolved around control and strict hierarchies. The phrase that many Germans grow up with is "trust is good but control is better." Insa found, as she studied the topic, that autonomy is one of the most important factors in ensuring a happy and productive workforce. People seek autonomy more than they seek responsibility, and the rise in start-up culture is a working example of this paradigm in action.

Insa is now the CEO of TheNextWe, an organisation that helps corporations implement autonomous and digitally minded company cultures that prioritise results over maintaining control. The companies that she works with have seen a huge spike in productivity and uptake of new digital tools. This demonstrates that Insa's hypothesis works even in the largest and most traditional companies.

The story is interesting and the concept important, but Insa's book title is the true stroke of genius in this example. Like Tim Ferriss' *4-hour Work Week*, *Der 2-Stunden-Chef* is intriguing, unusual and certain to garner media interest. Finding a similar hook for your own story is the most important factor in whether or not it will be picked up by media outlets. Insa's story was covered by numerous high-profile publications, which generated awareness for her company.

Journalists are under constant pressure to find stories that generate engagement. Clicks, comments and reactions are the key indicator of a successful story. But finding those interesting stories that haven't been told elsewhere is a difficult task. As someone who wants your story to be published, your main goal is to make the journalist's life as easy as possible: offer them a story that their audience will love, giving them maximum impact with minimal effort.

How do you do this on a practical level? I'm going to give you a step-by-step guide to guaranteeing positive media coverage that reaches the right people.

Step one is to nail down your key message and the most exciting aspects of your story, the things that other people will care about. This isn't about selling a product or a service, it's about telling a story that audiences can relate to. If people are interested in your story, they will want to find out more, and that's where the relationship building can begin. Media coverage creates a first touchpoint, an opportunity for people to understand your values.

Step two is to identify publications, blogs and podcasts that already attract your audience. Start with your dream ten or 25 outlets that you would love to be featured in and be ambitious but realistic. Your first article won't be in the *New York Times*, but it could be in a highly respected local business journal with strong regional readership.

You should always identify the right person to get in touch with. Sending emails to a general "info@company.com" address will get you nowhere. This also demonstrates that you have done your research and are seeking a genuine relationship. Journalists are often cynical about being pitched to. Bear in mind that the majority of emails that they receive are not relevant to their audience or their beat. You have to demonstrate that you have selected them specifically, rather than giving the impression that they are simply one name on a long list of many.

Here's a little insider secret from 20 years of working with the media: spend your time researching the journalist, their style, their audience and their usual content. With this information in mind, refocus your story and draw out the specific points that would be perfect for their style and their audience. Effectively, hand them a story that they could run tomorrow without any extra effort. Demonstrate that the hard work is already done, particularly how to make this story relevant to their readers. By putting in this work, you monumentally increase your chances of publication.

It is often easy to find the contact information for relevant people who work for podcasts, blogs and even smaller publications. Finding the contact can take a bit of digging for larger publications or broadcast stations. Here are some tips:

- Ask around. Maybe you know someone who knows someone, and they can put you in touch. A professional contact may have been previously featured and be in contact with an editor.
- Look for articles on a relevant topic and look for the name in the by-line. Once you have a name, you can call the office and ask to speak to them.
- When targeting a broadcast outlet, ask to speak to the producer of a particular show.
- Search social media. Journalists are generally on Twitter. Follow them and engage with their content and after a while, send them a personal message.

Now onto *Step Three*: pitching. Pitching is basically convincing whoever you are in contact with that they should publish your story. You should have a pitch ready both verbally and in writing so that you can quickly and confidently send something to a journalist when asked. Often, if you send a brief email outlining the initial idea and the journalist is interested, they will ask you for a pitch that summarises the story. This pitch should include a headline, key idea and the main points of the story, tailored to the journalists as I outlined above.

Focus on getting your first story. Once you win your first placement, you can approach the next journalist with greater credibility. But don't deliver the same pitch to the next journalist who expresses interest – they don't want to just recycle content used by their competitors. You need to find a brand-new angle or target an outlet with a different audience and have specific reasons why the story would be relevant for their demographic.

You can start small and work your way up. You can also focus all of your energy on one big catch, but this is likely to be a longer process, which entails building a relationship with a journalist over time and then eventually pitching the story with little idea if it will even be published.

The right tactic depends on how exciting your story is. Personally, I always try to aim high. This tends to improve the storylines I pitch, because I have to ask myself "how on earth can I get coverage in this publication?" Even if the story isn't picked up, this kind of thinking can help you to develop ideas that are exciting enough to generate interest from smaller publications, at the very least.

ENTER AN EXISTING CONVERSATION

Another way to gain the trust of journalists and to get your name out there is to enter an existing conversation by providing statements. The minute an event relevant to your industry occurs – be it the merger of two companies or the bankruptcy of an industry stalwart – reach out to the media with a few quotable sentences reflecting your opinion on the subject. Your aim is not to be self-promotional. You want to provide relevant insights quickly. Let them know what you think the future of your industry will look like because of that event.

Even if your media statement does not get picked up, you are showing the journalist that you can provide real-time insights into important events. They are much more likely to turn to you again for a comment in a pinch. Over time, this has the potential to turn into a mutually beneficial relationship. Some consultants have become the go-to sources for journalists covering a particular sector.

Celebrate your hard work: once you have gained coverage, share every story on your own channels, website and so on to boost your credibility. Tell other journalists that you have been trusted by a news outlet and that you would be pleased to contribute to their work too. In doing so, you develop a virtuous circle of the media improving your reputation, which in turn allows you more media coverage.

Generating media coverage is also excellent for SEO. Large media outlets are often at top of many search engine results, which means that your story is more likely to be seen by people who are searching for your name, your business or even the topic you spoke on. This can also give you access to an entirely new audience.

In the digital age, it's easy to believe that social media is the keystone of a great reputation. But traditional media should not be neglected. Anyone can create a social media account, but an article in a respected publication can offer you credibility that is unmatched by more contemporary media.

Once you establish a relationship with a journalist, you want to get published. Today journalists are under enormous pressure to produce several stories a day that prove popular with their audience. If you address this need, your chances of getting published increase considerably. Three ways to go beyond statements are op-eds, interviews and press releases.

Op-eds: Op-eds must be centred on a strong idea that is articulated clearly and concisely. If writing is not your strong suit, brief someone who can turn your thoughts into a coherent piece. Op-eds need to reflect your strong but well-founded opinion. Address the opposition but refute their argument and tell the audience why your position is correct. Before you send anything, open up a dialogue with the relevant editor.

Media interviews: Are you comfortable in front of a camera or being questioned by a reporter? If you shine when the spotlight is on you, try to book as many media interviews as you can. Interviews are difficult because they leave you vulnerable. But at the same time, the reward is high. Positive stories generated by interviews allow you to be seen as authentic and human. Less high-profile outlets and many online media simply send you a list of questions for you to answer in writing. This is way easier and more controlled than in-person interviews, which do require training and practice.

Press releases: They are an efficient way to reach numerous outlets, but rarely get picked up today unless they come from a big company or contain hard news. You have to craft something that is attention-grabbing and relevant. You can't be self-promotional. No journalist these days will read a release that starts with: "We are excited to announce…"

The best way to raise awareness with a press release is to send a relevant, interesting piece that places your news into a larger dialogue to a journalist with whom you have a relationship. Don't spray and pray. Rather select a smaller number of relevant journalists not to be seen as a spammer. Make sure to include some quotes so whoever you send it to can easily include it in their piece.

PUBLIC SPEAKING

Public speaking is daunting to many, but it is a skill and not a gift. Some of the greatest speakers, such as Steve Jobs and Michelle Obama, have honed and crafted their skill through constant exposure and practice. It can be a powerful tool for connecting with others. Public speaking is part of human nature: we have the desire to share ideas and to share stories. And speaking in public is as simple as that, you are just sharing ideas, stories and messages with an audience.

It might feel unnatural to be on a stage, but you can always start small. Try speaking in front of a small audience of family or friends. Just standing up, introducing yourself and sharing a few sentences about yourself is a great starting point. It will get you comfortable with speaking in front of an audience.

There is no need to reinvent the wheel. At this point in your personal branding journey, you have thought about how you want to present yourself. If you can stand up at a meet-up and state the values and messages that you formulated in week one, you are on your way to becoming a great public speaker.

Once you have graduated from meetups and smaller groups, the next stage is to tackle a panel discussion. These are often smaller, informal affairs, and it's much easier to talk in response to a question than to speak without a prompt. You also share a stage with other people, so you are one of three or four people sharing the responsibility of entertaining and inspiring others.

With a strong online personal brand backing you up, it will be easier to reach out to event and panel discussion organisers. If you have been presenting yourself as a thought leader, you will be the kind of person that they want at their events. Sometimes it is as simple as raising your hand and saying that you have something you want to contribute. Opportunities are out there. Go find them!

Panel discussions are great because you find yourself in front of an audience that is actively engaged in your topic. These are ideal individuals to connect with and get to know because you share an interest, values or industry expertise. Not only do you get a chance to meet these people, you meet them from the position of an expert. This is great for strengthening your personal brand.

The next step is booking your own speaking slots. These are opportunities to present your own ideas in your own way, at a conference or an event full of like-minded individuals. When you speak at those events, other opportunities will come to you: now that people can see that you are an expert in your field, they will want to get to know you and do business with you.

Great speeches are memorable, powerful and endure the test of time. "I have a dream" and "Ich bin ein Berliner" are speeches that continue to resonate to this day.

Great speeches tend to have one line, one key message, that people can internalise and emotionally connect with. I encourage anyone writing a speach to think of their one line, that one key message, that characterises what they would like others to walk away remembering.

A common pitfall of speeches is trying to include too much content and too many ideas. Keep it simple so that it's memorable.

Your one big idea should have emotional value. It should be a call-to-action or something helpful, informative and inspiring that your audience can use in their lives. I recently went to an outdoor stand-up comedy show in Berlin. The show was hilarious and engaging. But what I remembered most was a single line that the comedian delivered after a personal story: "Don't let anyone take your ice cream cone." This line symbolises self-care and not letting others take advantage of you. It resonated, and I remembered it.

Use this tactic in your own speeches. It is not your job to simply inform; it is your job to inspire. And that requires passion: if you are passionate about your idea, then others will buy into that passion and into your idea.

The best speeches have a clear, carefully crafted starting point: your attention hook. This could be a story that draws people in and develops an emotional connection. It could be a question or a broad claim. It has to be something that demands attention and that gives the audience the opportunity to follow a storyline. The middle of a speech should be conversational and free flowing. This is easier if you start from a strong, clear point. You are simply expanding on your ideas, as if you were explaining them to a friend or colleague. Finally, your call-to-action should rouse the audience, leaving them with a thought or an idea that they will continue to mull over when they leave the event.

It's important to practice your speeches. Deliver your speech to friends or colleagues. I find it useful to record my speeches with my phone and listen back to them to make any changes. This will allow you to look back and see what worked and what didn't, and most importantly, whether it was interesting.

Keep your speech short and sweet. Research suggests that we can listen to a single speaker for a maximum of fifteen minutes before we lose interest. You want to deliver a powerful message, not a boring university lecture. When you are first writing your speech, make it five minutes long. Make sure that those five minutes are powerful, flow clearly, and have a strong structure before you add anything else.

In terms of language, keep it simple. Make sure your audience can follow what you are saying and that they will take away your main message. If you are speaking to an international audience, ensure that non-native speakers can follow along. Don't use too many facts and figures. The only facts you include should be 'killer facts' that will highlight a point you are making or that the audience will remember. One number or one figure can clearly and memorably underline the point. These are facts that people will repeat to their friends later in the day.

Lubomila Jordanova, CEO and co-founder of Plan A, reminds us that "apocalyptic statistics don't work." As a CEO of a company that helps companies assess and mitigate their impact on the climate, she has to speak about complex topics. Even though her speeches are about climate change – a difficult, overwhelming topic – she uses positivity in speeches and across all communications in her company. Your job as a speaker is to make people feel empowered and excited.

Energy is vital. Audiences respond well to speakers who want to be in the room and want to share their ideas. An energetic speaker is an effective speaker. Find your energy switch. What activity pumps you up? Whether it's running around, shouting, jumping up and down, find something that gives you a boost of energy and do that each time before you give a speech.

Don't be afraid to use your voice. We can all think back to that maths teacher we had that droned on and on in a monotonous voice. Don't lull your audience to sleep. Change your pitch, rhythm and tone to emphasise certain points and to keep the audience's attention. In terms of body language, be dynamic. You should record yourself giving a speech and analyse your body language. Most of us may feel silly when we adapt our movements to keep attention. It may feel over the top, but trust me, it will appear natural when you are on stage.

Public speaking is a learnable skill. Practice really does make perfect here, so don't be disheartened. If you watch Michelle Obama's keynote address at the Democratic National Convention in 2008 on YouTube, she had little of the charisma that she is renowned for today. Her words are wise and she seems composed, but the contrast with her recent speeches is striking. In her most recent addresses and during her book tour, she simply seems born for the stage. Her presence, charisma and humour never cease to impress. To get where she is now, she put in hours and hours of practice. Practice, watch yourself, fix mistakes and keep trying. Everyone can excel at public speaking.

Don't build your personal brand in a void. Raising awareness is necessary, along with all of the other efforts I have shared with you, to create a robust, unignorable brand. Your hard work will pay off. You will become the person, online and offline, that your customers can't ignore. Your story will feature in the publications they read, on the social media they scroll through and at the events they attend year after year.

No matter how you raise awareness, always deliver value by informing, inspiring and entertaining. In other words: by giving. Bring value to your audience and to the journalists you are in contact with, and you will make yourself both remarkable and indispensable. As in all of the other vital tasks related to personal branding, keep the audience at the centre of what you are doing, and you will see positive results.

CONCLUSION

You've reached the end of your journey. Congratulations! I hope that you have a newfound sense of confidence, ease and satisfaction at the idea of becoming unignorable. At the start of this book, I asked you to write down what you will gain from building a personal brand and what you will avoid. Right now, I ask you to revisit those comments and add anything else that you have noticed since the beginning of this process. You will be amazed at how many benefits you will gain after even a few weeks of building this personal brand. Keep these lists at hand. As you progress in your career, they will motivate you and help you develop even further.

The entire exercise of personal branding can be incredibly fulfilling, if treated in the right way. It has been my mission to guide you through this process so that you feel empowered and excited by the new opportunities that lie before you. It is always worth taking a moment to reflect on where you have come from in order to contextualise where you can see yourself heading. Are you emerging from the shadows to become unignorable?

From finding your *why* to your key messages, from developing a content calendar, to learning the fundamentals of standing up on a stage and sharing your unique voice, I hope that you have found a brand-new sense of direction and a drive to reach your full potential.

With your strategy in place, you can make sure that the right people see your value. You will be unignorable. Remember that you can lose a job or business, but you can't be fired from your amazing reputation. While companies come and go, your skills are yours forever. By taking the time to curate an ecosystem, you are making yourself indispensable to the people that understand your vision and value your advice.

For a moment, let me draw your attention back to the statement that I laid out at the very beginning of this book:

To be seen, we must be visible. To be heard, we must have a voice. To make an impact, we must share our vision.

With the steps outlined in this book, you have found the emotional purpose behind your personal branding journey. You have realised what value you bring to others and learned how to write about it in a compelling way. You have nailed down your key messages and found a way to develop those messages into exciting content. You have started to find your audience. You have started to build meaningful connections that could already be turning into fruitful professional relationships.

An agile strategy that fits your goals will set the foundations of your brand. The tactics you have chosen to execute will move your brand forward. You now have a strong understanding of a wide range of personal branding tools that are at your disposal. You may even be considering book-writing, podcasting, media interviews and public speaking as the next steps forward. You know how to be truly seen as an expert in your field.

Most importantly, you have started to prove your value to the people who can truly make a difference in your professional life. With these steps, you are ensuring that you are never overlooked. You have found your voice, and you are making it unignorable.

You know how to take your brand to the next level. I recommend you always fully master one tactic or platform before adding something new. However, over time your tactics will become habit, and you will have much more space to experiment with new and exciting ideas.

Remember, this is not a vanity project. You are not an influencer; you are not trying to become a celebrity. You are a thought-leader. A true expert who solves pressing problems. If you truly provide value to those who matter, people will be lining up to do business with you. No one wants to be sold to. Instead, they want a trusted advisor and partner. You now have the tools to accomplish this. And you already know what feels authentic for you.

You have what it takes to be unignorable. The only thing left to do is start.

CONTINUE YOUR JOURNEY

Make the most of your personal branding journey by downloading the *Unignorable Workbook* at oliveraust.com/unignorable. The workbook is packed with exercises that guide you through the process and challenge you to think deeply about how you can become truly unignorable.

HAVE YOU HEARD?

The invisible don't build great businesses. The unignorable do. Hosted by Oliver Aust, the *Unignorable Podcast* is a series for all those who want to build a personal brand and share their unique voice with the world. In this series, Oliver expands on the topics he covers in this book and talks with some of the leading voices in the space. Learn more at oliveraust.com.

ACKNOWLEDGEMENTS

After having published two books in 2019, I did not expect to write another book the following year. Then two things happened: Firstly, the COVID pandemic put a lot of projects on hold so that windows of time opened up. Secondly, all around me there were (and are) fantastic people and businesses struggling due to the recession and ongoing restrictions. This is heart-breaking, and since I was in a similar tough spot during the financial crisis of 2008, I felt the urge to write down what I had since learnt about building a personal brand to boost your business.

For two decades now, I have worked with executives on enhancing the reputation they have worked hard to build. Once the pandemic hit, it became obvious that these same tools could be used by any professional to weather the storm, to make a career change or to secure their financial future. It is my sincere hope that this book will help many to thrive despite the crisis.

Of course, finishing a book about personal branding takes a lot more effort than simply writing down my insights. It is a big undertaking. It took a team, and countless hours of collaboration, to produce the book you have read. Two extremely talented wordsmiths, Isobel Hambleton and Sierra Stalcup, were instrumental in crafting this book with me. Without them, I doubt it would have ever seen the light of day. Vincent Wolff, Lena Carlson and Diane Vitry were indispensable in improving our initial drafts by asking the tough questions and making countless suggestions for improvement. Bianca Amorim Santos worked tirelessly to turn a pile of paper into a beautifully designed book. And Kristin Küter developed many ways how the book could find its way into the hands of interested readers. A huge thank you to the whole team!

The wonderful and inspirational Linda Broschkowski provided astute comments and insights, bringing up questions I had not even considered. Her love and support made this book possible, in so many ways.

My friend of two decades Bettina Hausmann, the best executive trainer and coach I know, identified numerous gaps in the draft caused by my own blind spots. I am incredibly thankful for her dedication to improving the models and methods in this book.

The foundation of this book lies in an online personal branding course I built with my team. Many of the concepts in this book were developed for that course, and so many of my colleagues and friends assisted me along the way to ensure we were creating the most valuable course for our members. I would like to thank Chris Armbruster, Edith De Santiago, Ben Griffiths, Monique Zytnik, Heike Rose, Akmal Kareem, Shirley Collet and Britta Lorenz for their insightful feedback on the course and suggestions for this book. The invaluable feedback they gave helped me stay on track and include answers to many questions that they brought up in recent months.

My sincere gratitude goes to all of them and the many friends and colleagues with whom I discussed the ideas in this book over many months.

I would love to hear from you on what you found useful about the book and where any future edition may be improved. Please get in touch at oliver@oliveraust.com.

USEFUL READING & RESOURCES

1,000 True Fans, Kevin Kelly (blog post)

Atomic Habits, James Clear

Building a Storybrand: Clarify Your Message So Customers Will Listen, Donald Miller

Fanocracy: Turning Fans into Customers and Customers into Fans, David Meerman Scott and Reiko Scott

High Performance Habits, Brendon Burchard

How to be successful, Sam Altman (article)

Messengers: 8 Ways to Get Heard, Stephen Martin & Joseph Marks

The Millionaire Messenger, Brendon Burchard

Oversubscribed: How to Get People Lining Up to Do Business With You, Daniel Priestley

One million followers: How I Built a Massive Social Following in 30 Days, Brendan Kane

Reinventing You, Dorie Clark

The Storyteller's Secret, Carmine Gallo

Start with Why, Simon Sinek

So Good They Can't Ignore You: Why Skills Trump Passion in the Quest for Work You Love, Cal Newport

This is Marketing, Seth Godin

Traffic Secrets, Russell Brunson

YOU MAY HAVE NEVER HEARD ABOUT

Personal branding is not something taken on only by well-known personalities. Here are some top-notch examples of individuals you may have never heard of who use LinkedIn for personal branding.

Dave Gerhardt – CMO of Privy

LinkedIn Followers: 70,143

David Gerhardt centres his brand on immediately practical advice that his connections can implement straight away. Posting several times a day, he shares his insights on marketing in short and easily digestible chunks. Reading through his feed, there is no fluff: each post is to the point and truly useful. Dave also exhibits a sense of humour in the way that he presents information. An example: "How to measure marketing 101: Sales. Have a good weekend."

Jessica Holzbach – Co-founder and CCO of Penta. Forbes 30 Under 30.

LinkedIn Followers: 6,187

Jessica Holzbach is a strong example of someone who keeps the personal out of her personal brand and is still highly successful. Her posting centres entirely on her company and on offering advice to other young founders. Her tone is professional and formal, but also very genuine and heartfelt. There is a clear impression left that you can trust anything that Jessica says: she speaks only when she has something truly valuable to add. An example of her posts: "Thank you. It feels weird to be called influential or "prägend." My whole attention span and focus goes into Penta, everything else somehow happens along the way. I always thought this is a bad thing, but as it turns out so far, focusing on one thing and doing it good, is better than 100 things okay."

Katie Kelleher – Crawler Crane Operator, LinkedIn Top Voice 2019

LinkedIn Followers: 18,988

Katie Kelleher is a perfect example of designing your personal brand to fit your personality, rather than trying to fit into a box. She is a female crane operator, and as such posts a lot about her day-to-day experiences and supporting women working in essential services. With her pink hair and red lipstick, Katie's posts are often more visual, prioritising videos and photos. She creates a very clear sense of her personality, offering an insight into a very unusual profession. Her audience is diverse and highly engaged because she offers a totally unique perspective on the platform.

Leena Nair – Chief HR Officer of Unilever. LinkedIn Top Voice 2018-9

LinkedIn Followers: 176,816

Leena Nair is a phenomenal ambassador for her company, as well as providing valuable content in a wide range of formats. From posts to podcasts, she seems to create whatever excites and interests her. Her brand centres around HR and helping people reach their professional goals. With a compassionate tone, many of her posts focus attention onto others in her network that are doing great things. She is a master when it comes to writing short, snappy hooks. A few examples: "What does a leader look like?" "Let's build a better business – and a better world." "This is the awful truth."

Yuval Atsmon – Senior Partner, McKinsey & Company, LinkedIn Top Voice 2016-19

LinkedIn Followers: 102,193

Yuval Atsmon leans into the world of data analysis in his personal brand, writing articles that use extensive research to make comments about the world today. His articles focus on business trends, economics and general global affairs, always offering an opinion but leaving the data for others to make up their mind. He often recommends books or podcast series, but that is the extent of his personal sharing. Yuval is a strong example of someone who keeps their personal brand wholly professional.

INDEX

ABOUT THE AUTHOR

Oliver Aust is one of Europe's leading communications and personal branding experts. He is on a mission to help people reach their full potential and share their unique voice with the world.

As founder and CEO of Eo Ipso Communications, he is a trusted advisor to many high-profile individuals and organisations.

He co-hosts a category-defining podcast on CEO communications, has written three books on the subject and shares his strategies in a blog on personal branding.

He has frequently been at the frontline of some of the most high-profile reputational challenges in Europe and he can draw on his personal experience of hundreds of media interviews as chief communicator for a publicly listed company.